BIBLE STUDY COMMENTARY

The Teaching of the
New Testament

Bible Study Commentary

The Teaching of
the
New Testament

DONALD GUTHRIE

Scripture Union
130, City Road, London EC1V 2NJ

CHRISTIAN LITERATURE CRUSADE
Fort Washington, Pennsylvania 19034

© 1983 Scripture Union
130 City Road, London EC1V 2NJ

First published 1983
Reprinted 1984

ISBN 0 86201 120 5 (UK)
    0 87508 179 7 (USA)

Phototypeset in Great Britain by
Input Typesetting Ltd., London SW19 8DR.

Printed in Great Britain by
Ebenezer Baylis & Son Limited
The Trinity Press, Worcester and London.

PUBLISHER'S FOREWORD

Since Scripture Union first published the *Bible Study Books* they have established themselves as a valuable aid to Bible Study. During their fifteen-year life they have been through several editions in a variety of formats and have enjoyed wide popularity in many parts of the world. When the time came to publish a new series (to be published under the series the *Bible Study Commentary* over the next four years) it was thought that its usefulness might be enhanced by the publication of additional books, giving important background material which lay outside the scope of the commentaries themselves.

When reading through a book of the New Testament it is not always easy to see how its teaching relates to that of the other New Testament writings. In this volume, Dr Guthrie gives a concise and orderly overview of the major doctrines taught in the New Testament.

His method is to take New Testament teaching subject by subject, looking at each area from the various perspectives of the writers of the synoptic Gospels, John's Gospel, Acts, the epistles, and Revelation. This not only helps us to 'interpret scripture in the light of scripture', and so ascertain the meaning of more difficult passages; it also reveals the unity of thought of the New Testament writers, so demonstrating the unique nature of the Bible as the inspired Word of God – a Word as relevant to the twentieth century as to the first.

CONTENTS

CHAPTER   PAGE

1 INTRODUCTION   9

2 GOD   13

3 THE CREATED WORLD   21

4 MAN AS A CREATURE   29

5 MAN AS A FALLEN CREATURE   37

6 JESUS CHRIST   43

7 THE KINGDOM OF GOD   59

8 THE ATONEMENT   67

9 THE HOLY SPIRIT   81

10 REPENTANCE AND FORGIVENESS   95

11 GOD'S INITIATIVE AND MAN'S
   RESPONSE   101

12 THE LAW AND THE COVENANT   111

13 THE CHURCH   117

14 THE LAST THINGS   129

15 CONCLUSION   143

1

INTRODUCTION

There are two main ways of approaching a study of the New Testament. In view of the fact that it contains twenty-seven books and is, in fact, a library of books rather than one book, it makes good sense to study each book separately. This has the advantage of enabling us to grasp the particular aim of each writer and to study his train of thought. Nevertheless it does not go quite far enough, for it tends to result in a number of fascinating cameos which do not necessarily at once reveal their close connection with each other. The complementary study of the whole New Testament is important precisely because it enables us to relate the teaching of each part to the whole. To obtain a clear picture of what the New Testament teaches it is necessary to extract from each of its parts the relevant teaching on its main themes.

This latter goal can be reached in two ways. One method would be to gather up the separate teaching of groups of writings, like the Gospels, the Acts, the epistles of Paul, but this method has not been adopted because it would still tend to leave us with unconnected groups. We have preferred to study the teaching of the whole New Testament under its major themes. In this way we have sought to produce a handbook of Christian teaching on those areas which are of most vital concern.

Some explanation is needed for the selection and arrangement of our themes. The total New Testament message may be summed up under the caption, *God and man and the relation between them*. But this broad subject needs splitting up into several divisions in order to answer some of the basic questions which have constantly been posed throughout the centuries. It is for this reason that a study of New Testament teaching has a continual relevance.

The first question we want to answer is, 'What is God like?' This will be the theme of our next chapter. We shall discuss the various ways in which God is described and outline some of his characteristics. We shall discover that the New Testament carries over the view of God which is expressed in the Old Testament, but brings out some features with much greater clarity. It presents Jesus Christ as the fullest revelation of God.

A study of God naturally leads into a study of the created order. We shall discuss the various ideas which are set out in the New Testament from the material creation to the world of men caught up in the present system. We cannot escape the conviction that God, the Creator, is sovereign in this world. We shall need to include in this study a discussion of the spiritual as well as the material world and this will introduce us to the kingdom of darkness.

The next question which arises concerns man's relation to God. The New Testament is uniform in seeing men and women in a state of need. Although there are many different expressions used to describe man's need, there is general agreement that man is alienated from God. A full appreciation of this situation is essential if the New Testament teaching about Christ is to have any relevance.

One of the key questions which every student of the New Testament wants to know concerns Jesus Christ. Who does the New Testament show him to be? How did his first disciples think of him? And what did he think about himself? How did the resurrection of Jesus affect the early Christians' understanding of him? The importance of the answers to these questions cannot be exaggerated. The Christian faith centres in Jesus Christ and an intelligent faith must pursue a quest for understanding him. We shall not be able to grasp the answer to the question of why God sent his Son unless we recognise that Jesus was both God and man.

When we enquire into what Jesus himself set out to do, we are obliged to make a special study of the kingdom because he so frequently referred to this. We shall examine those parables which deal with this theme and we shall also discuss to what extent Jesus expected a present or future kingdom.

Since in all the Gospels the events of the passion week occupy a remarkable proportion of the contents, it is important to discuss why Jesus died. On the surface it would appear to have been a tragedy, but none of the Gospel writers and none of the early Christians thought of it in that way. The New Testament makes very clear that the crucifixion was not an accident, but a part of God's plan. We shall note various ways in which it was explained and the way in which it continued to be an essential facet of Christian faith for the early church.

Our next consideration must be to study the work of the Spirit, both in the life of Jesus and in the life of the early church. There is no doubt that the Spirit plays a major part in the ongoing work of the community and in the lives of individuals. There is no subject on which it is more important for Christians to have an understanding of the New Testament teaching than this.

It is clearly vital to discuss how people became Christians in those days. This will lead us into a discussion on New Testament repentance and forgiveness. These are the initial experiences in the Christian life. We shall need to follow this up with some discussion on what the New Testament says about God's initiative in salvation and about man's responsibility.

Clearly there is more to the Christian life than its beginning and some study of what is expected of the believer is indispensable. Is he expected to be perfect? Is perfection indeed attainable? What resources are placed at the disposal of the believer? To what extent is the believer still bound by the law? These and other similar questions must be answered if there is to be growth in the Christian life.

But man was not intended to live in isolation and we shall consequently want to study the New Testament teaching on the Christian community. Life in community involves corporate worship. It also involves leadership and discipline and these are matters of concern to all serious students of the New Testament procedures.

A concluding set of questions affects the future destiny of believers. What evidence is there for life after death? How will the present age end? Is Jesus coming again? What will heaven be like? Is hell a reality? Some indication will be given of the New Testament answers to these questions.

2
GOD

Some people do not believe that God exists. Some would admit his existence but ignore his relevance to their lives. Some again have only a theoretical approach to him, being more interested in the intellectual arguments for his existence than in contact with him as a living person. But the New Testament introduces us to a personal God, who is not only very much alive, but is actively concerned with human affairs. The reader is not confronted with arguments for his existence, but is confronted with God himself in a way which makes the best possible sense of man and his environment. We shall outline some of the main teaching about God in the New Testament, but we must recognise that we shall fail to appreciate the force of it unless through it we experience the presence of God. There can be no nobler theme than this and no one should approach it without a sense of awe.

It is important to note at the outset that the New Testament view of God does not arise out of nothing. It is a continuation of the Old Testament understanding. It is not surprising, therefore, that the New Testament simply assumes that God exists and that he cares for the world, for this is the view presented throughout the Old Testament. It is true that in the New Testament some facets of God come into clearer focus, but there is no doubt that the God of the New Testament is the same God as in the Old Testament. The main difference that the coming of Jesus made to man's understanding of God is that God is brought incredibly near and is seen in action in Jesus in a way that finds no parallel in the Old Testament, except in the form of predictions of further revelations to come.

We may divide our present subject into two broad divisions – what God does and what God is. It will be obvious that in the nature of the case neither theme can be fully grasped, for the human mind cannot hope to appreciate the activity and attributes of God, as Paul notes in Romans 11:33–36. Nevertheless, God has revealed enough of himself for the mind of man to grasp and to wonder. What is knowable of God can only lead the thoughtful person to worship.

What God does

It is best to begin with the activity of God, for this avoids abstractions. Moreover, it is crucial to the biblical view of God that he is seen to act. His activities, moreover, are inextricably tied up with the welfare of men and are therefore far removed from exercises of mere power. We may sum up his major activities as creating, revealing, reigning, saving and judging.

God creates   This is certainly a basic assumption derived from the Old Testament. But there are several reaffirmations of it in the New Testament. The whole created order is seen as the work of God (Mark 13:19; Acts 17:24; Rom. 11:36; 1 Cor. 8:6). It also reveals much about the power and character of God (Rom. 1:20). It is a fitting theme for the heavenly worship of God (Rev. 4:11). Even in those days when man's knowledge of the physical universe was infinitesimal compared with his present grasp, the firm conviction that God created led to a profound understanding of the nature of God. There is no suggestion in the New Testament that the world came into being as a result of an accident. It is central to its whole message that behind the material world is a creating God. If the New Testament writers had a sense of awe in the presence of God the Creator, how much more should modern man with his increasing understanding of the vastness of space? But nothing that science has discovered about the universe has lessened the relevance of the New Testament conviction that God cares for the creatures of this earth which he has created.

We note that nowhere is any indication given of the manner of creation, except that it came into existence through the command of God (Heb. 11:3). But the fact that God created carries with it the corollary that God existed before his creation and is clearly distinct from it. This is why the New Testament speaks of God as being 'before the foundation of the world' (John 17:5,24; Eph. 1:4). But the most important fact in the New Testament view of the creative activity of God is that Christ was the agent of creation (John 1:3; Heb. 1:3) and also that creation was made for him (Col. 1:16). The significance of this is that when God created he had his own Son in mind. Man does not and never did own the world. If in his greed he destroys his environment, he is destroying what God made for his welfare.

Another aspect of the New Testament teaching is its emphasis on the providence of God. There is no evidence that God created and then left his creation to its own devices as the Deists maintained. On the contrary, God not only creates, but continues to care for his creation. Not even a sparrow falls without God knowing (Matt. 10:29). He cares for the birds and clothes the flowers (Matt. 6:26–31). But more important still, he concerns himself with the minutest details of human life (Matt. 10:30). He has a providential care for all men (Acts 17:25). Every endowment that man possesses comes from God (Jas. 1:17). Jesus taught his disciples to pray for daily bread (Matt. 6:11; Luke 11:3). There is a suggestion that a special providence operates for those who love God (Rom. 8:28), and this aspect will be further mentioned below when God's saving actions are discussed.

God reveals   We have already noted above that God is seen in his creation. But he is seen also in other ways. He is light, and darkness is wholly alien to him. As light he expects man to know the difference between the two and to reject the darkness (John 1:5–7). But the New Testament shows God revealing himself most perfectly through his Son (Heb. 1:3; Col. 1:15). Whoever has seen and known Jesus has seen God (John 14:8–11). The total work of God in Christ is therefore a revelation of God. Moreover, God is continually revealing his will to Christian people, who are exhorted to live according to it (Rom. 12:2). Throughout the unfolding drama of redemption, God has taken the initiative in making himself known. The New Testament lends no support to the view that man by his own effort can know God. There is not the slightest hint that God can be known except in the way that he has chosen to make himself known, i.e. through his creation and through his Son. Jewish thought increasingly saw God as remote, but the New Testament sees God as ever ready to communicate directly with man.

God reigns   Another of the dominant ideas of God in the Old Testament is that he is King. The people of Israel saw Yahweh not only as Creator, but as Sovereign. He was King over Israel and also ideally of the other nations. This idea is carried over into the New Testament particularly in the notion of the kingdom of God, which figures so much in the teaching of Jesus and will be the theme of a separate chapter later on. It is evident that this notion would have no meaning if God was not sovereign in his world. In his temptation, Jesus rejects at once, on the basis of scripture, the thought that the devil had any right to claim sovereignty over this world (Matt. 4:10; Luke 4:8).

The sovereignty of God is one of Paul's strong affirmations. No other powers are equal to God. He is greater than the rulers (1 Cor. 2:6–8) and greater than the principalities and powers (Rom. 8:37–39; Col. 2:15). Ultimately everyone and everything will be put under his feet (1 Cor. 15:24–26). God is declared to be King of the ages in 1 Timothy 1:17. A similar idea occurs in the anthem of the heavenly worshippers in Revelation 19:6, which fastens attention on the consummation of the kingdom. Indeed, the idea of God on his throne comes to focus not only in this book (Rev. 4:1–3), but also in the letter to the Hebrews (Heb. 1:3; 8:1; 12:2). It is also found in 1 Peter 3:22. This kingly activity of God is further supported by the ascription of the title 'Almighty' to him in the book of Revelation (compare 4:8; 11:17; 19:6,15), which gives some indication of the supreme power which is vested in God as he reigns throughout the history of this age.

God saves   With all the emphasis on God's power and sovereignty, there is another aspect which is certainly found in the Old Testament, but which again comes into clearer focus in the New Testament. The saving work of God centres around his concern for those who have rebelled against him. In the New Testament the idea of God as Saviour is found (for example, Luke 1:47; 1 Tim. 1:1; Tit. 3:4), but generally it is attributed to Jesus Christ. Nevertheless no distinction can be drawn between these ideas, for it is through Christ that God saves. This saving activity springs from the love and mercy of God (see below).

The idea of God as the compassionate Deliverer ties in with what is the most distinctive feature of the New Testament teaching about God, that is, the fact that he is Father. Not only did Jesus himself call God 'Father' (for example, Luke 10:21; John 8:28; 17:1,5,11), but he also taught his disciples to address God as Father (Matt. 6:9; Luke 11:2). There can be no doubt that for him it was a basic way of thinking about God. In the Old Testament God is seen as the Father of the nation of Israel, for the Israelites are frequently thought of as the children of God, and occasionally the idea occurs in a more personal sense. But in the approach of Jesus it is totally natural. Indeed when he used the familiar 'Abba' form in addressing God (Mark 14:36), he was introducing an intimate style of address which finds no parallel in the Old Testament. It stands out especially against the remote idea of God which was current among his contemporaries. It is difficult to imagine what the religious people of the time thought when Jesus was audacious enough to address God in this way. It is no wonder that his critics thought he was blasphemous. Yet this was the most far-reaching and exciting idea of God that man had ever known. From then on the disciples of Jesus could rest assured that their Father knows their needs (Matt. 6:32). God, as heavenly Father, may be relied on to have more care for his children than human fathers have for theirs (Matt. 7:9–11).

One aspect of God's fatherhood which must be mentioned, is its relation to his creatorship. Is he the Father of all men in the same sense in which he is the Father of believers? In what sense, if any, does the New Testament think of him as universal Father? There is a sense in which God as Creator has brought to birth every creature, but in the special sense in which the New Testament thinks of the new birth (that is, as spiritual salvation), his fatherhood applies only to those who through faith have become sons of God (John 1:12). This must mean that in their ongoing life Christians find in God the source of life and spiritual power. Throughout the New Testament we find God continually being addressed as Father. It should be noted, however, that the risen Jesus makes a distinction between God as his Father and God as the Father of the disciples (John 20:17). In a special sense Jesus was Son of God in a way that no one else is. Nevertheless, the relation between Jesus and his Father is frequently seen as a pattern for his disciples (compare John 17:21,23).

God judges   We might have included this function of God under his kingship. But it is better to think of it in close connection with God's saving power. It is a less attractive aspect, but is nevertheless essential. If God has defined his standards, he must pass judgement on those who deliberately reject them. Jesus set out this sterner side in many ways, and no one questioned it (compare Matt. 7:1,2; 11:22–24). Paul is equally emphatic that God must judge (compare Rom. 2:16; 3:6). In one statement the apostle links the severity of God with his kindness (Rom. 11:22). There is no support in the New Testament for the view that God is a tyrant. His acts of judgement are everywhere based on justice. God's kindness shows that mercy tempers his judgement. But the New Testament picture of God is of one who is fully holy as well as being fully loving.

What God is like

Having noted the main activities of God it is now possible to enquire what he is like. No final answer can be given, but the main characteristics stand out with some clarity. The life and actions of Jesus are said to reflect God's *glory* (Luke 2:20; Mark 2:12; Matt. 15:31), and this characteristic of God is attested in several statements in other parts of the New Testament. Indeed, so convinced is Paul that God is a glorious person that he calls him on one occasion 'the Father of glory' (Eph. 1:17). In several doxologies glory is ascribed to God (for example, Rom. 16:27; 2 Cor. 4:15). Jesus Christ is a reflection of God's glory (Heb. 1:3). In the worship sections of the book of Revelation, God is portrayed in figurative language as a glorious being.

Another characteristic of God is his *wisdom*. This is in strong contrast to the wisdom of men (1 Cor. 1:20). Although much of God's wisdom is necessarily beyond the reach of man, much has been shared with man (Eph. 3:10). Paul can declare that Christ is 'our wisdom' (1 Cor. 1:30). The wisdom of God implies his perfect knowledge. Nothing can be unknown to him (Matt. 10:26). In fact, perfect knowledge also involves foreknowledge, which Paul mentions in Romans 8:29. This understanding of God's wisdom is extended in the New Testament to the choices made by God, especially in terms of those people he chooses to be his servants (compare Eph. 1:4). Although many have stumbled over the problem of predestination and God's free will, the New Testament writers never saw it as a problem, only as an evidence that God is wise in all his ways.

Further comments will be made about the problem when considering man's response, but for our present purpose it must be noted that the New Testament teaching is that God's intentions are always perfect, his words are always dependable, he cannot lie (Tit 1:12) or prove false (Heb. 6:18). This is why so much emphasis is laid on the fulfilment of the will of God (compare 1 Cor. 1:1; Rom. 15:32; Heb. 10:36). Jesus is himself the perfect example of acceptance of the will of God (Matt. 26:39). Even suffering could be considered as being according to God's will (1 Pet.

4:19). In spite of the problems this raises, acceptance of the perfect will of God is seen to be the most desirable aim for the Christian (Rom. 12:1,2).

Closely allied to the fact that God is all-knowing is the clear assumption that he is *perfectly holy* (John 17:11). He is worshipped as the Holy One in the book of Revelation (4:8; 15:4; 16:5). Moreover, he is also *righteous*, which means that he always acts in a just way and also expects righteousness in others (Rom. 10:3). This quality is the basis of his judging. Although holiness and righteousness are closely linked they must be distinguished. God's character is without blemish and he cannot therefore act in an unrighteous way. Because of this he cannot show partiality (1 Pet. 1:17; compare Heb. 6:10). There is no doubt that this aspect of God is over-aweing, but it cannot be side-tracked for that reason. It is a necessary part of the total New Testament picture of God.

We close this brief survey with a note on the most characteristic quality of God in the New Testament, that is, his *love*. This love is seen supremely in the Father's love for his Son (John 3:35; 5:20; 10:17) which then becomes the pattern of his love for men (John 17:23). Paul frequently appeals to God's love as the motive for his saving activity (Rom. 5:5–8; 8:39). The sending of the Son is said to be because of the love of the Father (John 3:16). The God of love is also a God of *grace*, a God who gives his favour to those who in no way earn it or deserve it. This quality of love does not, however, conflict with the quality of holiness. They are different sides of the same quality. God's love is holy love and his holiness is so pure that it is perfect in love. The two qualities are inseparable.

3

THE CREATED WORLD

The New Testament is more concerned with man as a creature than with the rest of the creation, but it is valuable to enquire what information it supplies about the world in general before turning to man in particular. It will be most convenient to discuss this in two sections, the material world and the spiritual world. But before setting out what the New Testament says on these themes, it will not be amiss to make some comments on the contemporary world view at that time.

Background ideas
In the Old Testament there is a firm belief that the material world came into being by a specific creative act of God. The Old Testament does not give any details of this original material world, apart from the fact that order emerged out of chaos. There is no suggestion that God did not continue to have a powerful interest in the world he had created. The fact that the Genesis account affirms that God surveyed his creation and pronounced it good shows that it originally conformed to his pattern. The biblical story deals with man's fall and restoration and the way in which the material creation was implicated in this.

Jewish beliefs in the intertestamental period were in line with Old Testament beliefs. There was a continued conception of the world as created. Moreover, in both periods there was a further conviction that supernatural forces, some good and some bad, were constantly at work behind the scenes.

It was in the Greek world that the idea was current that the material world was inherently evil. This affected the world view and led to the belief in a good principle and an evil principle. This dualism was taken over by the gnostics, but is not supported in the New Testament, which not only affirms that God is sovereign in his world, but that evil is rooted in man's mind, not in his material environment.

The material world

Our first consideration must be to enquire what view of the world the New Testament writers had. We must at once recognise that the writers lived in a time when understanding about the physical world was severely restricted compared with our modern knowledge. The expressions used reflect their own times. While this must be admitted, it is relevant to ask whether the New Testament actually teaches anything about the physical universe which is plainly untenable in the light of our modern scientific enlightenment. Does the New Testament, for instance, depend on a theory which supposes that the earth is flat? Is the basic premise that the earth is the middle storey of a three-storied universe, sandwiched between the heavens and the nether regions? The following evidence will go some way to showing that these theories, which were widely current in the first century, are not demanded as the New Testament understanding of the world.

There is surprisingly little information in the Gospels about the physical world. Although the word 'world' occurs often, it is generally used of the world of men. The world is seen as the forum for the preaching of the gospel (Matt. 28:19). In the parable of the tares the field is the world (Matt. 13:38). The needs of the 'world' present a challenge to the gospel.

Is there any evidence that Jesus thought that the earth was flat? Did he imply this when he spoke of 'the four winds' of the earth (Matt. 24:31)? It would be precarious to argue from this what Jesus' world view was because the context demands no more than a reference to the four points of the compass. There is no statement in the New Testament which clearly affirms a flat earth and it is therefore impossible to say what the writers believed. The same may be said about the three-storey theory. The fact that Jesus is said to have ascended 'up' into heaven (Acts 1:11) may belong to language which thinks of heaven as 'above' the earth, but it is difficult to see in what other way the complete withdrawal of Jesus in a physical sense could be demonstrated. The 'up' and 'down' language may be used to describe the incarnation and ascension of Jesus without necessitating acceptance of a three-tier universe.

It is more important to note that the Gospels show that the 'world' is under the influence of evil (compare Matt. 4:8), but this is different from the Greek view of the evil of matter. The dominance of Satan is in the moral world. It is for this reason that the 'world' comes to mean, especially in John's Gospel, that which is opposed to God. In John 1:10 the evangelist states that when the light came into the world, the world did not know him. Here 'world' is clearly used of the world of men, and this is the sense in which God is said to have loved the world (John 3:16). The biblical focus is everywhere on man and his relationship to God rather than on the physical world.

In noting Paul's teaching about the world, we find the same emphasis on the moral aspect (Rom. 3:6; 1 Cor. 6:2; 11:32), but it is worth pointing out a few statements which have a bearing on his view of the physical creation. He sees the whole created order as having been made by, and for, Jesus Christ (Col. 1:16). This means that he looked at the whole creation from the point of view of Christ. He even goes as far as to think of the whole creation groaning as it waits for its ultimate redemption (Rom. 8:22, 23). Generally speaking, however, the world for Paul is the world of men who are alienated from God. Nevertheless, the apostle offers hope because God has reconciled the world through Christ (2 Cor. 5:19). At the same time, he is clear that Christians, while still living in the world, should not live as if they belonged to the world (Col. 2:20). We may conclude that Paul, in common with other New Testament writers, shows considerably more concern with the world as the arena of man's activities than with the question of the origin and character of the material creation.

In Hebrews there is a direct reference to the Creator resting after having completed his creation of the world (Heb. 4:4) and in the same epistle Noah is said to have condemned the world (Heb. 11:7), another example of the double use of the term. Rather more specific references to the utter dependence of the physical world on God are found in Revelation, especially in the use of the title 'Almighty' in reference to God (compare Rev. 1:8; 4:8; 15:3; 19:6).

The spirit world

We are entering into a supernatural sphere when we begin to talk about angels and demons. It is a different area of discussion from the physical world. The latter can be seen and it is therefore regarded as legitimate to ask questions about it. But when angels and demons are discussed, many would at once feel that these belong to a world view which is no longer applicable. Our concern, however, is not with the question whether a belief in angels and demons is tenable, but whether the New Testament asserts their existence. After examining the evidence we will be able to see its relevance to our modern age.

Even on a cursory reading of the New Testament, the importance of angelic agencies in the unfolding of God's activities is undeniable. We are at once confronted with angel intervention in the narratives about the birth of Jesus (compare Matt. 1:20,24; 2:13; 2:19, where an angel of the Lord is mentioned, and Luke 1:19, 26 where the angel Gabriel is named. Compare also the heavenly host in Luke 2:13). Jesus declined to call for the help of angels in Gethsemane, although he clearly had power to do so (Matt. 26:53). The expression 'before the angels of God' is sometimes used to denote the presence of God (Luke 12:8; 15:10). Jesus also refers to guardian angels for children (Matt. 18:10), but nothing more is said about their function.

Another major event which features angels is the resurrection of Christ. An angel appears at the tomb (Matt. 28:2–7; John 20:12), and a report circulated that the women had seen a vision of angels (Luke 24:23). Again, angels are mentioned in connection with the return of Christ (Matt. 16:27; 25:31; Mark 8:38).

There is no doubt that angels form an essential part of the Gospel narratives and their significance cannot be ignored. The same emphasis is found in Acts, where angels are mentioned in connection with several important events. An angel releases men from prison (Acts 5:19; 12:7–11). Again, an angel of the Lord gives instructions to Philip (Acts 8:26) and to Cornelius (Acts 10:3–8). During the storm at sea Paul receives a message through an angel (Acts 27:23). In Acts 23:8 there is a passing reference to the fact that Sadducees did not believe in angels, an opinion which was not, however, shared by the Pharisees.

Paul provides little evidence on the subject of angels, but there is sufficient to show his firm belief in their existence. He speaks of himself as a spectacle to angels, as if they have a special interest in what the apostle is doing (1 Cor. 4:9). He forbids the worship of angels (Col. 2:18). In 1 Timothy 3:16 he says of Christ that he was seen by angels. He links angels with the presence of God (1 Tim. 5:21. He mentions that the law was given by angels (Gal. 3:19). In looking ahead to the return of Christ he predicts that he will come with angels (2 Thess. 1:7). He even appeals to the angels as a reason for his teaching regarding women (1 Cor. 11:10,11). There can be no doubt that he believed in the existence of supernatural agents who were acting in some way, which he does not define, as God's servants.

The letter to the Hebrews is even more emphatic in its acceptance of angels. The first two chapters are devoted to establishing the superiority of Christ over angels. There is a comparison between Christ as Son and the angels as ministering spirits (Heb. 1:4–8,14). There is also an innumerable company of angels in heaven referred to in Hebrews 12:22.

The idea that angels have a real interest in man's salvation is appealed to in 1 Peter 1:12. Peter also sees them as subject to Jesus Christ (1 Pet. 3:22). More light is shed on what angels do in the book of Revelation. Several times announcements are made by angels with loud voices (Rev. 5:2; 10:1; 18:1; 19:17). Their purity and dignity are seen in the description of them as robed in white and girdled with gold (Rev. 15:6). Many of the judgements are carried out by angels (compare Rev. 8:2; 15:1; 16:1). They are said to surround the throne of God. One of the leading angels is named in Jude as the archangel Michael (Jude 9).

This New Testament teaching about angels is so strong that its testimony to their existence is indisputable. The same applies to the existence of spirits of evil. All the agencies of evil are gathered up into one supreme person, Satan. He appears on the scene at the temptation of Jesus (Matt. 4:1–11), he is said to have bound a woman for eighteen years (Luke 13:16) and to have entered into Judas prior to his betrayal of Jesus (Luke 22:3). He is seen to be active in Peter when the latter tries to resist the purpose of Jesus (Matt. 16:23). Jesus recognised the powerful influence of Satan and assured Peter that he had prayed for him (Luke 22:31). This shows the measure of the intense spiritual conflict in which Jesus was engaged. Satan is recognised as the ruler of this world (John 12:31), who is nonetheless a defeated foe. Another aspect of Satan is his promotion of falsehood and murder (John 8:44).

In view of this it is not surprising also to find in the Gospels a considerable number of cases where people are said to be possessed by demons which were cast out by Jesus or his disciples. The demons are variously described as 'unclean' or 'evil' (Mark 1:23; Matt. 12:43,45). Demon possession is said to cause various physical ailments (Matt. 12:22; 15:22) and to display considerable violence (Mark 5:1–13). It must, however, be noted that the Gospels make a clear distinction between illnesses and demon possession. Sometimes the demons witnessed to the character and power of Jesus (Luke 4:34; Mark 5:7), but he rejected such testimony.

Outside the Gospels we find the same firm belief in the activity of demons. The agency of evil comes in Acts 5:3; 13:10; 26:18. The most notable instance was Satan entering into Ananias. Moreover, demons were cast out by various people (compare Acts 5:16; 8:7; 16:16–18; 19:12–16), which shows a continuation of the same conditions as those which applied during the ministry of Jesus. The early church is seen as a liberating agency through which God was breaking through the captivating power of the spirit world.

Paul is a witness to the reality of these adverse spiritual forces. He recognises Satan's hindering activity (1 Thess. 2:18). He knows that he creates tension (2 Cor. 2:11) and harasses the servants of God (2 Cor. 12:7). Paul even speaks of defectors being 'delivered to Satan' for the good of their souls (1 Cor. 5:5; 1 Tim. 1:20). Satan can transform himself into an angel of light (2 Cor. 11:14), but his real business is to blind men's eyes to the gospel (2 Cor. 4:4). Paul is under no illusion about the power of this enemy of the truth. He warns the Ephesians to beware of his wiles (Eph. 6:11).

Paul is equally aware of the hosts of darkness. He speaks of 'principalities and powers' and it is almost certain that by these he means evil agencies (Rom. 8:38, 39; 1 Cor. 15:24). Christ, however, is superior to them (Eph. 1:21). In addition Paul has some references to demons, as, for instance, in connection with idol worship (1 Cor. 10:19–22). He also refers to doctrines of demons (1 Tim. 4:1). Moreover, he seems to regard the rulers of the present age as being under the control of evil agencies when he describes Satan as the god of this world (2 Cor. 4:4). Again, there is no doubt about Paul's awareness of the spiritual conflict facing the Christian church. Yet he is equally convinced that following the coming of Christ the adverse spiritual world has been conquered.

One aspect of the devil's activity is particularly brought out in Hebrews 2:14 where he is described as having the power of death. This fits in with Jesus' description of him as a murderer. There are specific exhortations to resist the devil in James 4:7 and 1 Peter 5:8. In the latter case, he is described as a roaring lion. It is, however, in the book of Revelation where Satan and his hosts meet their final overthrow. Satan is named several times (compare Rev. 2:9,13,24; 3:9; 12:9; 20:2,7) and is also referred to under other names (*diabolos*, dragon, serpent, deceiver). He is seen as the powerful counterfeit of all that is good and as the direct antagonist of Christ and his people. It is in this book of visions of judgement that the reader discovers that, despite the wide influence of evil agencies, their power is limited, for God and the Lamb will finally overcome.

4

MAN AS A CREATURE

There are various approaches to the New Testament teaching about man. Some consider that the New Testament is an account of man's search for God, in which case it becomes man-centred. But such an approach, if carried to its logical conclusion, gets no further than man's present understanding of himself and rules out the idea of revelation. It must be recognised that God not only reveals himself in the New Testament, but makes a revelation of what man by nature truly is. It may not be a flattering picture, particularly in the insight it gives of man's sinful condition. But it is precisely because it presents a completely unbiased picture of man that the New Testament evidence is so valuable.

The perfect pattern

Much confusion can be avoided if, in a study of man, we take the ideal pattern as the starting point. The only way to do this is to look at the human Jesus who is everywhere seen in the New Testament to be *perfect man* (see section 6). It is important that we do this rather than concentrate on Jesus becoming *man as we are*, because he came to show us what *true manhood ought to be*. We see him in the Gospels as kind and unselfish, as concerned for the welfare of others, as totally dependent upon and obedient to the Father. It is in John's Gospel that this latter theme is particularly stressed. He is seen as sent from the Father (John 3:16) to work the Father's works (5:17,19), to do his will (6:38), to be one with the Father in every respect (10:30). This sets before us the highest possible pattern for man. It seems totally *im*possible, but no New Testament view of man would be in the least complete or adequate which did not take into account that this ideal portrait of man *is* in fact possible, because Jesus lived his life in that way.

We notice especially that Jesus provides an example in his attitudes towards others, especially towards those in need (compare John 5:14; 9:35–38). How very human he was is seen in his approach to the problem which arose at a village wedding (John 2:1–11), or in his response to the Samaritan woman (John 4:7) or the hungry crowds (John 6:5–11). His weeping at the grave of Lazarus (John 11:35) shows him as a person of high sensitivity and compassion. The same may be said of his concern for his mother while he was on the cross (John 19:27). It is against this background of perfect manhood that we must study various aspects of man in the New Testament. This comes out in such passages as Hebrews 4:15, where our High Priest is said to know our weaknesses, although he did not succumb to them. He is further seen as an example in 1 Peter 2:21, in which context Christians are urged to follow in his steps. In all probability Paul implies the same in Philippians 2.

Man in creation

In line with the Old Testament view, the New Testament sees man as a created being. Jesus, moreover, recognised God's care over his creation and considered that man was of more value than other creatures in creation (Matt. 10:31). This is in agreement with the Genesis account, which puts man in a superior position to animals (Gen. 1:26).

Because of the fact that man has been created by God, he has an obligation to obey his Creator. This is brought out, for instance, by such a statement as Acts 5:29, where man is said to have a prior obligation to obey God rather than his fellow men. The duty to obey God is deeply ingrained in the Old Testament and may be said to be assumed in the New Testament (compare Acts 7; Heb. 3,4). A corollary of this is that all men are on the same footing before God. This is of great importance in connection with racial issues. There is no distinction between the Jew or Gentile in respect of man's position before God (Gal. 3:28). This is remarkable in the face of the strong antagonism beween Jew and Gentile in the contemporary world. It is fundamental to the New Testament view of man that racial distinctions have no relevance. God shows no partiality. The basic equality of all men springs naturally not only from the fact that God is Creator of all men, but also from the fact that the redemptive activity of Christ embraces men of all nations.

Jesus made some remarkable statements about the infinite value of man in the sight of God. To be told that the hairs of each person's head are all numbered (Matt. 10:30) vividly illustrates this truth. Jesus moreover reckoned that a man's soul was more valuable than gaining possession of the whole world (Mark 8:36). Such a saying shows unmistakably that man is more important as a spiritual person in a right relation with God than as a person owning possessions. In a materialistically dominated age, men would do well to reflect on the New Testament scale of values, which puts materialism low on the list. We may further note that the Gospels' presentation of Jesus as becoming man to save men underlines the infinite worth of man in God's sight (compare John 3:16).

The New Testament view of man must be seen against current Greek ideas of the possibility of the deification of man. The New Testament writers lend no support to this idea. Some have supposed that 2 Peter 1:4 (speaking of men as partakers of the divine nature) is along this line, but this statement cannot be isolated from the rest of the New Testament. It must be understood in the Christian sense of believers becoming sons of God.

Man's nature
The New Testament uses a variety of different words to refer to man and these form a cumulative picture of what he is.

Body   Man has a body, which denotes his physical side. The body (Gk. *soma*) is described both as mortal (Rom. 8:10,11) and yet as capable of being transformed through the Spirit. It is never described as evil, as the Greeks believed it to be. In the Christian life the body is even regarded as a temple of the Holy Spirit (1 Cor. 6:19). A stronger contrast to the Greek idea could hardly be imagined. It is possible to glorify God in the body (1 Cor. 6:20). The body, therefore, although affected by man's fall is as much the object of the saving work of Christ as any other part of man. It, as well as the mind, needs to be dedicated to God (Rom. 12:1,2). But to do this the deeds of the body need to be put to death (Rom. 8:13). It is because of the importance of the body in the Christian life that Paul is so definite about the future resurrection of the

31

body (2 Cor. 5:1–11) – which will be commented on later in the chapter on 'the last things'.

Flesh   Another word which is closely linked with body, but with a distinctive meaning, is flesh (Gk. *sarx*). Sometimes the two words are used interchangeably (for example, 1 Cor. 1:29; Rom. 1:3), but more often in Paul 'flesh' represents man in his weakness and implies a sinful bias. It is because of this that Paul can speak of 'the mind of the flesh' (Rom. 8:5,6), that is, a mind set on activities of the flesh. Mostly, 'flesh' is linked with sinful desires or sinful acts (Gal. 5:16,19). In one passage Paul describes his own struggles against the flesh, but rejoices in deliverance through Christ (Rom. 7). When compared with the word 'body', 'flesh' has an implication of evil which 'body' has not. It should be noted that this strong moral sense which is attached to 'flesh' is the reason why Paul so often contrasts it with 'spirit'. In no other New Testament writer does this contrast have such weight.

Soul and spirit   There has been much discussion over the distinction between soul and spirit; both of these terms also occur frequently in Paul's epistles. Of the two, 'spirit' (Gk. *pneuma*) is used many more times than 'soul' (Gk. *psyche*). The latter word usually stands for a man's life or self (Rom. 11:3; 16:4; Phil. 2:30). Man consists of soul and body (Matt. 10:28) but the word 'soul' is used of the whole person (compare Matt. 16:26). When Paul thinks of the soul he sometimes implies its sinful bias (compare Rom. 2:9). One passage in 1 Thessalonians (5:23) calls for comment since it implies that man has a three-fold nature, body, soul and spirit. But it must be remembered that Paul is here describing a Christian man, and his words cannot be taken generally to define man's constitution. It is better to suppose that 'spirit' relates to the awakened state of the regenerate man, in which case it is an inappropriate expression for man in his sinful state. This explains the frequency with which Paul contrasts flesh and spirit.

When we consider the New Testament view of man as spirit, we are again mainly dependent on Paul's epistles. He sees the Christian man as a new creature (2 Cor. 5:17). It is the Holy Spirit who witnesses to man's spirit (Rom. 8:16), which shows that a distinction is made between them. There are occasions when Paul may be using the word 'spirit' to refer to self (as in 1 Cor. 16:18), but generally he uses it of man's higher nature which has been revived by the Spirit of God. The spiritual man (1 Cor. 2:15) is the man who has the mind of Christ. His soul and body, that is, the whole man, are brought into relationship with God.

We may wonder where such a concept as 'mind' comes into the picture. The mind is unquestionably an important part of man's constitution according to the New Testament. It can be dominated by the flesh (Col. 2:18), but it is not necessarily bad. It can be blinded by Satan (2 Cor. 4:4), but can also be enlightened (2 Cor. 4:6). For the Christian the mind can be renewed (Rom. 12:2). Indeed, the potential of the mind of man is to be conformed to the mind of God. Struggles unavoidably come to the mind of the Christian man as tension arises between his unregenerate state of mind and his mind now set on higher things (Rom. 7; compare Col. 3:2). There is no suggestion in the New Testament that the intellect remains unaffected. In man's natural state the mind is incapable of appreciating spiritual realities. The natural person is one whose thoughts are in no way controlled by God.

Conscience   In considering the subject of man in the New Testament, we must mention the place and function of the conscience. All men have consciences through which they become aware that they are rational beings. Paul maintains that the Gentiles, who did not have the Jewish Law, had consciences (Rom. 2:15). This suggests that all men have the capacity to know the difference between right and wrong. In this context Paul does not give any indication of the standard used. He is concerned rather to establish that men have no excuse. It is possible to disobey conscience and when this happens over a period of time it becomes 'hardened' – insensitive and self-justifying (1 Tim. 4:2). When in this state, it can be called 'evil', as in Hebrews 10:22. A hardened conscience can be brought to 'life', that is, back to a working moral awareness, through the Spirit. It should be noted that the conscience of man in general does not pronounce that man is evil. It is only the awakened conscience of the Christian which recognises this. Nevertheless, the conscience of the non-Christian does tend to make him aware of his sin. When he becomes a Christian he discovers God's forgiveness, and his conscience becomes 'clear' (1 Peter 3:21) – that is, it becomes free of guilt feelings. Recognition that man has this capacity to determine what is right or wrong not only gives him dignity as a creature, but also imposes on him responsibility for his actions.

Male and female   No survey of man in the New Testament would be complete without a discussion of sex. The doctrine of man must include some comment on the distinction between male and female and the relation between them. When the attitude of Jesus towards women is considered, a remarkable contrast with the contemporary situation is at once seen. Judaism was male dominated, and the pagan world generally regarded and treated women as inferior to men. Yet in the accounts of Jesus' life women played a significant part. Mary the mother of Jesus is described as the most favoured of women (Luke 1:30). Although Jesus did not choose any women apostles, a group of women accompanied him on his travels (Luke 8:1–3). He spent time with the outcast woman of Samaria (John 4), allowed a sinful woman to touch his feet and anoint them with ointment in face of Pharisaic criticism (Luke 7:36–50), and appeared first to a woman on Easter day (John 20:11–18). Indeed, women figure prominently in the passion narratives. It was the women who took spices to embalm the body. Moreover, women feature in many of the parables told by Jesus (especially in Luke). Both in his actions and in his teaching Jesus acknowledged the dignity of women. When compared with the contemporary Jewish view of women, the approach of Jesus was revolutionary.

In the early church no distinctions were made when the Spirit descended at Pentecost; women were numbered among the disciples (Acts 1:14). Joel's prophecy, cited in Acts 2:17, mentions daughters as well as sons prophesying. Lydia plays an important part in the founding of the Philippian church and many leading women were among the believers at Thessalonica (Acts 17:4) and Berea (Acts 17:12). This evidence shows a continuation in the early church of the liberated view of women which is seen in the attitude of Jesus.

It has often been supposed that Paul is rather harder on women, but this is not a true reading of the evidence. It is he who makes the categorical statement that in Christ there is no distinction between male and female (Gal. 3:28). It is worth noting that he links this rejection of any distinction between the sexes with the sweeping away of any distinction between racial groups (Jew, Greek) or social groups (slave or freeman). It is clear that different relationships existed in the Christian and non-Christian world. The coming of Christ made a profound difference in the status of women. There is no suggestion in Paul's epistles, or in any other part of the New Testament, that the basis of salvation for women was any different from that for men. It is important to note that in dealing with the relation between the sexes Paul condemns the homosexual practices of contemporary Roman society (Rom.

1:26,27). He recognised that the sexes were complementary to each other (1 Cor. 11:8,9; compare Eph. 5:31; 1 Cor. 11:11,12). In one passage (1 Tim. 2:9–14) he seems to be adopting a view supporting male domination on the basis of an interpretation of the Genesis account of Eve. Although this passage declares that it was Eve, not Adam, who was deceived, yet in Romans 5:12–14 and 1 Corinthians 15:22, Paul lays the origin of sin squarely on Adam. On the question of women in the New Testament church we shall make further comments in a later section.

Family life   There is no doubt that the New Testament takes a strong line on the sanctity of marriage and the value of home life. Paul gives specific advice to husbands and wives, and also to parents and children. There is no suggestion that he or any other New Testament writer would have countenanced an easy attitude towards divorce or towards the break-up of the family. Jesus had shown a warm regard for children and had used a child as an example for his disciples (Matt. 18:1–14). This tender approach was in contrast to much of the harsh treatment of children which was characteristic of some sections of the ancient world. Again, the coming of Christ had brought into human society a more humane touch.

Jesus was concerned about the conditions in society around him, although he was in no sense a social reformer. He taught that man must be concerned about others. He was not intended to be an island. The disciples of Jesus were expected to be 'light' and 'salt' in the world (Matt. 5:13–16). They are exhorted to be peacemakers (Matt. 5:9). Jesus himself showed great compassion towards the deprived (Matt. 11:4,5) and commended those who showed social concern for others (Matt. 25:31–46).

5

MAN AS A
FALLEN CREATURE

In our last section we considered man as a creature, but we must now move on to think of him in relation to God and this at once leads us to a study of the New Testament themes of sin and judgement. It does not require a revelation to convince us that mankind is imperfect, but revelation is certainly necessary to make clear the nature of the imperfection and the serious consequences of it.

The nature of sin
In the New Testament there are many different words used to describe man's failure and some comment is needed on the various distinctions which these words bring out. The most common is the word for sin (Gk. *hamattia*), which covers a whole range of actions which are contrary to God. Man is seen as a sinner when he has failed to measure up to God's standards or when he has deliberately set himself at variance with God. When John the Baptist preached repentance, it was in relation to sins (Matt. 3:6), and the idea of God providing remission of sins, which is introduced here, is followed through in the rest of the New Testament revelation. This general word for sin is used in the words of institution at the last supper, where the blood of the covenant is said to be poured out 'for the remission of sins' (Matt. 26:28). No understanding of what Jesus came to do is intelligible apart from

THE TEACHING OF THE NEW TESTAMENT

the recognition of the fact that man is a sinner. The very name of Jesus is said to signify that he will save his people from their sins (Matt. 1:21).

The earliest call to repentance by the apostles on the day of Pentecost was connected with the general word for sins (Acts 2:38). Paul records that Christ died for our sins (1 Cor. 15:3; Gal. 1:4). Although the word is generally used in the plural, there are some important statements which speak of sin in the singular, thus gathering up into one term the whole sequence of man's offences against God (for example, John 1:29; Heb. 9:26; 13:11).

It is, however, the variety of other words used to describe man's condition which throw most light on his relationship to God. Such words as evil (Gk. *ponēria*) and wickedness (Gk. *kakia*) show an aspect of sin which is morally intensely undesirable. Evil is the opposite of good and wickedness is a deliberate attitude of malice which represents the antithesis of God's designs for man. Both are totally alien to the nature of God.

Lawlessness There are other words which describe specific aspects of sin. Sometimes sin is specified as lawlessness (Gk. *anomia*. Compare 2 Cor. 6:14, where RSV 'iniquity' would be more accurately translated 'lawlessness'). The antichrist, who is the personification of all that is against Christ, is called 'the man of lawlessness' (2 Thess. 2:3). This is an assessment of sin seen against an accepted standard of law. If God's demands are set out in terms of legal requirements as they are in the Decalogue, then it follows that any failure to match up to these requirements must be regarded as against the law. Lawlessness in Paul's use of the word does not describe inadvertent acts of law breaking, but a deliberate and persistent policy of going against God's law.

Deviation This rejection of God's demands is found alongside another view which sees man's failure in terms of trespasses (Gk. *paraptoma*) (compare Mark 11:25; Rom. 4:25). The idea here is of a deviation, a stepping aside from the right path. This can be less deliberate than lawlessness, although the end result is equally a lack of alignment with God's pattern for mankind. The man who strays from the right path thinks he can map out his own route independent of God.

Indebtedness In the Lord's Prayer the disciples of Jesus are taught to ask for forgiveness of their debts (Matt. 6:12), where it is clear that the debts denote sins. The same idea is probably found in Paul's epistles, for example in Colossians 2:14 where Paul uses a word which may mean 'a certificate of indebtedness' which has been cancelled through Christ. It is a corollary of the high view of God in the New Testament that man is placed in God's debt. Not only is this true in respect of his creaturely status, but also in respect of his failure to meet God's just requirements. This sense of debt led in the intertestamental period to the idea of merit in God's sight which could be earned, and which could in some way help to counterbalance the indebtedness. But the New Testament knows nothing of this idea.

Slavery Another figure of speech which is used of sin is that of slavery. This is powerfully brought out in Paul's epistles. Indeed, Paul regards sin as a taskmaster (Rom. 6:16,17). Slaves have no rights and Paul sees sin as reducing people to complete bondage. It is part of his presentation of the gospel that Christ has brought freedom. Jesus spoke of himself as a ransom (Mark 10:45), which suggests the purchase price needed for the freeing of a slave. One of the dominant ideas in Paul's theology is that Christ's death brought deliverance (this is the root meaning of redemption). It is clear that the significance of this theme will be grasped only by those who acknowledge their bondage. Those who declared they had never been in bondage to any man (John 8:33) were completely incapable of appreciating Jesus' statement that the truth would make them free.

Ignorance A rather different assessment of sin is found in relation to knowledge. It is in John's Gospel that the notion of sin as ignorance comes to the fore. Those who do not know the truth walk in darkness. Jesus is seen as light (John 1:4–9; 8:12), which the darkness did not comprehend. In 1 John 2:11 it is darkness that has blinded the minds of those who hate their brethren. Paul writes in the same vein of those whose minds are blinded by Satan (2 Cor. 4:4). But does this mean that man's plight would be rectified by more knowledge? Is salvation no more than an educative process? The New Testament gives no support for such a view, but there is no doubt that man in his sin is in a state of ignorance which can be alleviated only through the light of the gospel.

Alienation Certainly sin brings with it alienation from God. Paul can speak of men as enemies of God (Rom. 5:10), which means that a barrier has been erected between man and God which, until it can be removed, prevents fellowship. This sense of hostility is summed up by Jesus as the hatred of the world (John 7:7). Sin has caused such ravages that it has resulted in hatred of God instead of love.

Unbelief So far the various aspects of sin mentioned have all been in relation to God the Father, but there is one important aspect which relates directly to Christ, and that is unbelief. At first sight John 15:22 might suggest that sin consists entirely in a wrong attitude to Christ. This would not, however, be a right deduction as the evidence above has already shown. There is no doubt that the coming of Christ has created a new situation which has extended the sphere of sin by including within it the lack of a proper response to God's revelation in Christ. The Christian era has seen a believing minority in the midst of an unbelieving environment. Whether or not a person believes in Christ may not be the sole yardstick, but a heavy responsibility rests on those who have been confronted with the claims of Christ. Those who know God but do not honour him as God are condemned by Paul (Rom. 1:21).

One aspect of sin which is particularly emphasised by Paul is its connection with flesh. This is complicated by the fact that he does not always use the word 'flesh' in the same way. Nevertheless when he contrasts flesh and spirit, he always thinks of 'flesh as affected by sin'. He could therefore speak of believers as having crucified the flesh with its passions and desires (Gal. 5:24). The connection between flesh and passions reminds us that the New Testament gives several lists of vices, in which immorality and other sexual sins invariably play a major role. Paul makes clear that the mind that is controlled by the sinful nature of flesh is hostile to God (Rom. 8:5–8), and contains nothing good (Rom. 7:18).

The scope of sin

We have seen sufficient evidence of the serious view which the New Testament writers take of sin. There are certain further features which will repay our attention. The first of these concerns the scope of sin. Are any exempt from it or is it universal? As far as man in general is concerned, we may let Paul answer our question, for he wholeheartedly endorses the Old Testament statement that all have sinned and have fallen short of God's glory (Rom. 3:10,11,23). No one is excluded from this statement. It forms the climax of Paul's argument in Romans 1–3, where he is demonstrating that both Gentiles and Jews are equally affected. It is all the more significant in view of this that Paul explicitly exempts

Jesus Christ from the charge of sinfulness (compare 2 Cor. 5:21). The writer to the Hebrews is also convinced of the sinlessness of Jesus (compare 4:15; compare also 7:26). It is the universality of sin in all others that marks out the uniqueness of Jesus. No one apart from him ever perfectly fulfilled the will of God. His example proves that such perfection is possible and justifies the righteous judgement of God on all imperfection.

It is on the basis of the universality of sin that Paul can maintain the contrast between Adam and Christ in Romans 5:12–21. He is quite clear that Adam's sin has affected the whole race and accepts the fact that death which comes to everyone is the result of sin. This deep conviction of the universality of sin is central not only to Paul's theology, but to the whole New Testament teaching. Nowhere is there any thought that anyone might through his own efforts throw off the damaging effects of sin. Indeed, the New Testament idea of salvation is based on the fact that everyone needs deliverance from those effects.

Accountability for sin

An important question is whether man is accountable to God for his sin, or whether he might reasonably argue that he had no choice since he was created with the possibility of sinning. But the New Testament lends no support to the view that God is responsible for man's sin. At the conclusion of his discussion in Romans 1–3:20, Paul affirms that the whole world is held accountable to God (3:19). Later on in the same epistle, he thinks of God as a potter and denies the clay any right to question the way it has been shaped (Rom. 9:19–21). But the analogy must not be allowed to reduce to nil man's responsibility for his own sin. The fact is that man is everywhere in the New Testament condemned for his acts of sin, which would make no sense if he were not accountable for those sins.

There is no doubt that the theme of judgement is crucial for a right understanding of man's relation to God. The sense of the natural man's alienation from God, which pervades all the New Testament teaching, focuses on the barrier which sin has erected. Fellowship with God became impossible while a state of hostility existed. But judgement involves more than the recognition of a barrier. It involves condemnation, an announcement of guilt (compare Rom. 5:16). This is clear from the New Testament view of the wrath of God. It is Paul again who has most to say on this theme, although it is by no means absent from the rest of the New Testament. Indeed, he maintains that in the same way that the righteousness of God has been revealed so has the wrath of God (Rom. 1:17,18). God's wrath is directed against all ungodliness and wickedness of men. Paul speaks of a day of wrath to come in the future (Rom. 2:5). This day of wrath will be the same as the day when Christ comes to be glorified in his people (2 Thess. 1:9,10). It is in view of this that Paul can describe the Ephesians in their former state as children of wrath like the rest of mankind (Eph. 2:3). God's wrath is turned against all unrighteousness because he is himself righteous. His wrath is not something alien to his nature, but is essential to it.

According to John 3:18 anyone who does not believe in Jesus is condemned already. This shows that faith in Christ is the only way to avoid the guilt of sin. We are confronted here with a double truth – the impossibility of avoiding the consequences of sin apart from Christ and the seriousness of the state of unbelieving people. The New Testament has much to say about the need for purification from the defilement of sin (in Hebrews this is a major theme). The aim of the gospel is to enable believers to be presented faultless before the throne of God, thus removing not only the obstacle between God and man, but also the guilt feelings of those who know they have fallen short of God's standard (1 Thess. 3:13). In the vision of the New Jerusalem there is no place found for anything or anyone unclean (Rev. 21:27). A major part of New Testament teaching is devoted to the theme of God's provision of a way for overcoming the condemnation of sin.

6

JESUS CHRIST

One of the most important questions which arises from the New Testament is 'Who was Jesus?' It is clearly not sufficient to state in answer that he was a Galilean peasant, for this would leave so many of the details of his life and death completely unexplained, but would also leave as an enigma how the Christian church ever came into existence. It is necessary to make a careful examination of many aspects of New Testament teaching before arriving at a considered answer to our question. We shall certainly need to consider Jesus the man, but we shall also need to go beyond this in discovering what Jesus thought about himself and what others thought about him.

Our first section will deal with Jesus as a human being. It is essential to know that he shared our humanity, for otherwise he could not be identified with us. We shall then think of the most important titles that Jesus used of himself and that others used of him.

Before doing this we must note how important it is to recognise that Jesus was a historical person. Because there are practically no details about the life of Jesus outside of the Gospels, some have raised doubts about the reliability of these accounts on the grounds that the records have come from those who had already believed certain things about Jesus. But even if all the witnesses were Christians this does not detract from their testimony. Indeed it may be maintained that their belief that Jesus himself was the Truth would predispose them to produce accounts which were based on true facts. No wedge must be driven between the faith of the early Christians and the facts about the historical Jesus. The Jesus who lived in Palestine was the same person that the Christians believed to be Lord, and Son of God.

Jesus the man

When we come to the Gospels we find accounts which mainly focus on the ministry and death of Jesus, and which include few indications of his life before the commencement of his preaching work. Apart from the birth stories of Matthew and Luke, which will be referred to later, the only incident prior to the baptism of Jesus is the occasion of Jesus' visit to the Temple at the age of twelve (Luke 2:41–51). Although the heavenly voice at the baptism shows Jesus to be different from other men, yet the fact that Jesus was baptised by John the Baptist indicates a deliberate intention to be identified with others who were coming for baptism (Matt. 3:13–17). Further, the baptism was followed by a period of temptation which showed Jesus in common with other men being subjected to moral challenges, although the special temptations which Matthew and Luke record are unique to Jesus (Matt. 4:1–11; Luke 4:1–13). This tension between Jesus as a real man and yet as a special man runs throughout the New Testament, but it cannot be said that the writers are particularly aware of it. Certainly the first three Gospels show Jesus as living and working among a first–century community in Palestine, with its religious and political environment, many features of which are reflected in the accounts, such as the scribes and Pharisees and the economic conditions of the time.

When we turn to John's Gospel we are again faced with a paradox, for although he begins his Gospel with thoughts about Jesus as God (see further discussion of this below), he nevertheless includes several indications of the real humanness of Jesus. He could become weary (John 4:6) and could be thirsty (John 4:7; 19:28). He could weep at Lazarus' tomb (John 11:33–35) and could be deeply troubled (compare John 12:27). John is clearly intent on showing Jesus as a real man.

What is true of the Gospels is also true of other parts of the New Testament. The early preachers frequently referred to 'Jesus of Nazareth' (for example, Acts 2:22; 3:6). In Cornelius' house Peter talked about God anointing Jesus of Nazareth as one who 'went about doing good', even after he had already declared Jesus Christ to be 'Lord of all' (Acts 10:34–43). There was a close connection between the Christ who was being preached and the Jesus of the Gospels. There is no doubt that he was one and the same person.

When we examine Paul's epistles we find little specific evidence that he was acquainted with the life of Jesus. But it would be wrong to suppose that he considered the human Jesus to be unimportant. Certain facts had been handed on to him (1 Cor. 15:3; 11:23), which show that his Christian faith was based on the historical life of Jesus. Moreover, he alludes to the poverty of Jesus (2 Cor. 8:9) and mentions his meekness and gentleness (2 Cor. 10:1). Although the apostle is more interested in the risen Lord, there is no suggestion that his exalted view of Christ has lessened his humanity. In the important passage in Philippians 2:6–11 about Christ, there is an explicit statement that Christ took on 'the form of a servant' and became obedient to death.

One of the clearest passages to focus on Jesus the man is Hebrews 5:7–10 which seems to be a clear allusion to Gethsemane with its mention of Jesus' strong crying and tears. In the same epistle he is said to have shared flesh and blood like his brethren (Heb. 2:14) and it is evident that the writer attaches great importance to the humanity of Jesus. He is concerned to demonstrate that Jesus has been subjected to testing like other men (Heb. 2:18; 4:15). It is important for the main thesis of this epistle about Jesus as High Priest to show that he was well qualified to act as a true representative of man in general.

In most of the other New Testament books the humanity of Jesus is assumed rather than stated. In the book of Revelation, for instance, the exalted Jesus appears as a Lamb, but the Lamb is nevertheless a slain Lamb, and this must relate to the historic death of Jesus. We may conclude that the New Testament gives no support to the view that Jesus was anything less than a real man. It gives the lie to the later view that the real Christ was the heavenly and not the earthly person. Whatever other view of Jesus is presented in the NewTestament, his humanity must be regarded as an essential constituent of the total picture.

If the true humanity of Jesus is necessary in order to identify him with the rest of mankind, it is important to show in what sense Jesus as a man is unique, distinguished from other men. There is no doubt that the most important aspect of Jesus' unique manhood is his sinlessness.

Although in the synoptic Gospels Jesus does not specifically claim to be without sin, it is wholly in harmony with the way he is presented. Nowhere does he confess sin. The nearest he comes to it is in his identifying of himself with those who were undergoing the baptism of repentance of John the Baptist. Yet even then there is no suggestion that Jesus was repenting as a sinner, and John's hesitation, which is specially mentioned by Matthew (3:14), does not suggest that he baptised Jesus on the grounds of repentance. Indeed, Jesus himself regarded the act as fulfilling righteousness rather than repentance. It is moreover to be noted that Jesus condemned sin in others (for example, Matt. 23) without any awareness of shortcomings of his own. There is no suggestion that anyone could have brought a charge of hypocrisy against him.

In John's Gospel there is one specific challenge made by Jesus to his critics, that is, 'Which of you convicts me of sin?' (John 8:46). No accusation was made except the jibe about being a Samaritan and having a demon, a complete evasion of the question. It is remarkable that in John's Gospel Jesus frequently claimed to be doing the will of God and yet no one was able to charge him with being hypocritical. When at his trial his accusers charged him with being an evildoer (John 18:30), even the pagan Pilate pronounced him innocent (18:38).

When we go outside the Gospels we find more than one specific statement that in Jesus there was no sin (2 Cor. 5:21; Heb. 4:15; 1 John 3:5; 1 Pet. 2:22). In each of these statements there is an undeniable reason for stressing the sinlessness of Jesus. It comes in 2 Corinthians 5:21, immediately after the extraordinary statement that God made Jesus 'to be sin for us', which must mean that he took our sins on himself although he had no sin of his own. In the Hebrews passage this concept of his sinlessness qualifies the statement that Christ was tempted in every way as we are. In 1 John 3:5 it is attached to the saying that Jesus came to take away sins, and a similar context is seen in 1 Peter 2:22. These statements are sufficient to show the considerable theological importance of the sinlessness of Jesus. Only a representative of mankind who had shown such perfection could deal with the root cause of man's failure. Only one who was righteous and totally obedient to the will of God could restore to fellowship those who are unrighteous and rebellious. It is essential to recognise therefore that Jesus the man was clearly distinguished from all other men in his purity and sinlessness.

Some have supposed, on the grounds of Romans 8:3 and Hebrews 2:17, 18, that at the incarnation Jesus took on sinful flesh. Only so, it is alleged, could he be like his brethren. But no view of Jesus becoming man which denies his sinless nature could adequately account for the evidence outlined above. It is clear that the humanity which Jesus possessed was humanity as God intended it to be in contrast to fallen human nature. Apart from dealing with the sins of fallen man, Jesus himself shows a perfect example of a new kind of human existence which had never been known before, since Adam's sin plunged the whole race into a state of rebellion.

Jesus the Messiah

There were widespread expectations in the Jewish world prior to the birth of Jesus that a special messenger of God would come to save his people Israel. Such a hope finds its footing in the Old Testament although there is little mention of a Messiah. Certainly a coming age was forecast by the prophets in which blessings would come to the people of God. The word 'Messiah' literally means 'the anointed one'. It came to be used of the hoped-for deliverer who would be set apart for this purpose in a way similar to the anointing of kings and prophets for their particular roles.

Another kindred idea to that of Messiah was expressed in the title 'Son of David'. The Old Testament hope of one to restore the house of David was based on 2 Samuel 7:12–16 and there are many allusions in the Old Testament to the coming Davidic king (for example, Jer. 30:9; Ezek. 34:23,24). In fact David came to be regarded as a representation of Israel as a restored community. As applied to Jesus in the New Testament, the 'Son of David' title must therefore be seen to be closely linked to the idea of Jesus as Messiah.

During the inter-testamental period, the messianic hopes developed along various lines. In some of the literature a heavenly being was expected, and in other instances an earthly figure who would overcome Israel's enemies. The latter idea seems to have been the predominant one, in which case the Messiah to come was to be an essentially political figure who would inaugurate the new age by means of military force. It should be noted, however, that linked with this view was an essentially religious idea of the coming deliverer. When he came he would be God's man and in God's strength would overcome Israel's enemies.

It was undoubtedly this political expectation of a Messiah which led Jesus to avoid using the title 'Messiah' of himself. All the same, on the occasions when he was addressed as Messiah he did not deny the ascription. Instead of the title 'Messiah' Jesus preferred the title 'Son of Man', presumably because it was free from political connotations. It is for this reason that the importance and significance of the Son of Man title will be considered in this section. As far as the Old Testament evidence is concerned the most likely source of the Son of Man title is Daniel 7:13,14 which refers to 'one like a son of man' coming to 'the Ancient of Days'. In the inter-testamental period only a few incidental references occur, which do not help us much in determining what the title meant to Jesus. For this we are restricted to the Gospel evidences.

We are now in a position to discuss what the Christian church meant when it identified Jesus as the Christ (that is, the Messiah). So widespread is the use of the title 'Christ' in the New Testament that it demands an effective explanation. Its precise meaning for the Christian is of great importance for a right appreciation of the New Testament view of Jesus, although it presents only one aspect among many.

In the Gospels we may note first of all the occasions when others use the title 'Messiah' and Jesus does nothing to refute it. His response to Peter's confession that he is 'the Christ, the Son of the living God', is positive (Matt. 16:13–20). He recognises that this could have come only as a result of revelation. Nevertheless Jesus did not allow his disciples to make known that he was the Christ. When he was asked by Caiaphas whether he was Messiah, the Son of God (Matt. 26:63), Jesus again does not deny it. It seems evident that he did not announce himself as Messiah simply be-cause, had he done so, most of his hearers would have supposed that he was setting up as a political deliverer. In John's Gospel the descriptive title was used by the first disciples and by the Samar-itan woman (John 1:41; 4:25). In the latter case there was no fear of a political understanding of the title, since the messianic expec-tation was not current among the Samaritans. It is important to note that John's purpose in writing his Gospel was to lead people to faith in Jesus as Messiah and Son of God (John 20:30,31). Clearly this is not to be interpreted as political messiahship, but a new and spiritual kind of messiahship.

When the apostles first proclaimed the gospel after the death and resurrection of Jesus, his position as Messiah (again in a spiritual sense) was acknowledged. The first announcement to this effect is found in Acts 2:36. The idea that Jesus was the Christ appears to have been an early confession (Acts 5:42). In his first preaching Paul makes the same declaration (Acts 9:22). Indeed, there are many instances of this in Acts (compare 17:3; 18:5; 18:28). Jesus, in these instances, certainly claimed to be a deliverer, but the apostles had in mind deliverance from sin, not from the Roman yoke.

The epistles are full of references to 'Jesus Christ' or 'the Lord

Jesus Christ' or simply 'Christ', which show that the messianic ascription has now become a proper name. When Paul uses it he knows that the messianic mission has already been accomplished. For him the Christ is the powerful spiritual deliverer. In the epistle to the Hebrews the emphasis falls on Jesus as High Priest rather than Messiah, but the title 'Christ' also occurs with some frequency.

It seems reasonable to conclude that the early Christians rec-ognised in Jesus the one who was expected in the Jewish world, although the idea was interpreted in a very different way. It is also reasonable to suppose that Jesus, with his knowledge of Old Testament teaching, thought of his mission in terms of the messianic hope even though he did not explicitly declare it and did not permit any such announcement by the disciples.

Son of David   As we have already noted, the idea of Messiah is closely linked with the title 'Son of David' because of the widespread belief that the Davidic kingdom would be restored. We find that both the genealogies of Matthew and Luke respectively show Jesus to be descended from David. Clearly the expression 'Son of David' would be entirely appropriate for Jesus from the point of view of human descent. There appears to be some popular use of the title reflected in Matthew's Gospel (compare 9:27; 12:23; 15:22). It is not to be concluded, however, that popular opinion necessarily identified the coming Messiah with the Son of David. When Jesus entered Jerusalem, he was met with the cry, 'Hosanna to the Son of David' (Matt. 21:15). In John's Gospel some were arguing that the Scripture maintained that Messiah was to be descended from David (7:42).

In the Acts and the epistles the evidence that Jesus was thought of in terms of the Son of David is slight. Although there is a strong affirmation of this by Peter in Acts 2:25–36 and by Paul in Acts 13:22–41, there is little evidence in Paul's epistles. In Romans 1:3 Jesus is said to be 'descended from David according to the flesh', and in 2 Timothy 2:8 a similar belief is reflected. Apart from this the only other reference in the New Testament is to Jesus as 'the Root of David' (Rev. 5:5; 22:16). From this slight evidence we may conclude that 'Son of David' was not regarded with as much importance as 'Messiah', but it nevertheless adds some royal dignity to the latter idea.

Son of Man   We have noted that because of the political associations of the messianic title Jesus declined to use it. In its place he used the title 'Son of Man'. It is remarkable that, in the Gospels, no one else used it of him, and this suggests that it must have had a special meaning for him. All the Gospels recount statements in which Jesus uses the title. Sometimes it seems to be a substitute for 'I', as for instance in Mark 2:28. At other times Jesus uses it when he is referring to his coming death, as in his predictions after the tour of Caesarea Philippi (compare Mark 8:31; 9:12,31). In yet other sayings Jesus is looking ahead to his return (compare Mark 8:38; 13:26; 14:62). A question arises over what Jesus meant by this title. It is certain that, in all the sayings where 'Son of Man' occurs, Jesus is referring to himself and he must have had a particular reason for preferring to describe himself in this way. The most probable explanation is that he is drawing attention to his humanity and to his being *par excellence* man's representative. It is also significant that Jesus could speak of the suffering Son of Man, but the idea of a suffering Messiah would have been totally unintelligible and unacceptable to his Jewish audiences. Moreover, the Son of Man in the Gospels is not a tragic figure, but a triumphant one. In John's Gospel there is particular mention of his glorification (John 12:23; 13:31). Even when 'lifted up' (that is, on the cross) he would draw men to him (John 3:14).

It is remarkable that the disciples, with one exception, did not use the title 'Son of Man' when referring to Jesus either in their proclamation or in their writings. The only one to use it was Stephen, who described seeing a vision of the Son of Man on the occasion of his martyrdom. No doubt the reason why the title completely dropped out of Christian use was because more explicit titles were available which could be used without restraint after the passion.

This may be a convenient place to mention the virgin birth, since this is in some ways linked with the title 'Son of David' considered above, although it also has significance for other aspects of the Christian understanding of Jesus. The importance of Jesus as man has already been made clear. But the New Testament undoubtedly shows that in becoming man he had a supernatural birth. Both Matthew and Luke record that Jesus was born of a virgin (Matt. 1:23; Luke 1:34,35), although it must be admitted that the New Testament elsewhere is not so specific about the virgin birth.

Jesus, Lord and Son of God
If the emphasis in the last section fell on Jesus the man, in this section we shall find less stress on his human life and more on his

risen life. Indeed, it would be of great value at this juncture to comment on the New Testament teaching about the resurrection of Jesus and its implications, for our next titles are inextricably bound up with this event.

All the Gospels have some account of the resurrection, although there are many details which are recorded by only one Gospel. It is difficult, but not impossible, to piece the four accounts together. What stands out vividly in the Gospels is that the evidence for some extraordinary event is indisputable. It cannot be explained away as the imagination of visionaries who wanted to believe, and therefore convinced themselves that it was true. Admittedly Jesus had predicted it (compare Matt. 16:21; 17:22,23; 20:19), but there is no evidence that any of the disciples grasped the significance of Jesus' predictions. It was rather the reverse. They were completely baffled by the death of Jesus, even though this was also predicted in specific terms at the same time. Nevertheless the resurrection predictions show that Jesus foresaw his conquering of death as an indispensable part of his mission.

It is not surprising to find that the event of Jesus' resurrection exerted a profound effect on the early church. Indeed it may be said that the only adequate explanation of the remarkable trans- formation of totally disillusioned disciples into bold proclaimers of the Gospel is the conviction that Jesus had risen. The apostles recognised that only those who had been a witness to the resur- rection of Jesus would be eligible candidates to replace Judas (Acts 1:22). This must mean that the one selected must have been among those to whom the risen Christ appeared between Easter day and the ascension. In the recorded speeches of Peter the resurrection is always mentioned as a historical event immediately after the mention of the death of Jesus (compare Acts 2:23,24; 3:14,15). It was not until after the resurrection and ascension that the Spirit was given to enable the disciples to grasp the full significance of that event.

In the epistles the resurrection is central. Paul devotes a whole chapter to it in 1 Corinthians (ch. 15), as well as making numerous other references to the fact that God raised Jesus from the dead (compare Rom. 1:4; 8:34; Gal. 1:1; Eph. 2:6). There is no doubt that the event of the resurrection is basic to Paul's theological position. But this is not simply Paul's opinion, for other New Testament writers are equally strong on this theme (compare Heb. 13:20; 1 Pet. 1:3,21; Rev. 1:17,18). Even in those books which do not spe- cifically refer to the resurrection, it seems to be assumed (compare James 2:1 – where the description 'Lord of glory' occurs; and 1

John 1:2 where the mention of life implies the conquering of death). It may be said that the strong affirmation of the resurrection affects the way in which the Christians thought about Jesus Christ. Titles were needed which adequately expressed the exalted nature of the resurrected Christ.

It is also important to remember that the resurrection is closely linked with the ascension to which it naturally leads. Although it is only Luke's Gospel and the book of Acts which include accounts of the ascension, there are indirect allusions to the theme in the teaching of Jesus recorded by John (3:13; 6:62; 20:17).

Generally in the New Testament the idea of the ascension is expressed in terms of the exaltation of Jesus. This was proclaimed in the Acts speeches (2:33; 5:31). Stephen saw Jesus at the right hand of God (7:55). Paul assumes the ascension in Romans 10:6,7 and Ephesians 4:9,10; but in Philippians 2:6–11, where the resurrection is not mentioned, the exaltation of Jesus marks the climax of his statement about Christ. This theme of Christ's exaltation is frequent in Paul (compare Col. 3:1; Rom. 8:34). Again, the book of Hebrews often describes Christ as being at the right hand of God (1:3; 8:1; 12:2). In this epistle the exaltation is linked with the intercession of Christ the High Priest on behalf of his people (compare 4:14; 7:26). In 1 Peter 3:21,22 the same theme of exaltation occurs, while the whole of the book of Revelation centres on the exalted Christ. It is against the background of the resurrection and ascension of Christ that the titles 'Lord' and 'Son of God' have to be interpreted.

Lord   The title 'Lord' was used in a variety of ways in the world of the first century AD. It could mean no more than a title of respect, in the sense in which 'Sir' is sometimes used in modern times. It could also be used of emperors (as Lord Caesar) or of pagan gods (as Lord Serapis). On the other hand it is used regularly in the Greek version of the Old Testament for God. It would be natural to expect that when the title is used in the Christian church for Jesus Christ something of the Old Testament usage is in mind.

We shall not expect much evidence from the Gospels that the title 'Lord' had any particular significance before the resurrection of Jesus. Indeed, the pattern seems to be one of non-theological usage before the resurrection, and theological use afterwards. When Luke wrote his Gospel he frequently referred to Jesus as 'the Lord', as he as a Christian had, no doubt, come to regard him. There is one instance where Jesus tells his disciples to refer to him as 'the Lord' (Luke 19:31), but it was not until he rose from the dead that the title 'Lord' was invested with special meaning for the disciples. The most remarkable use of this title in reference to Jesus was by Thomas when he linked it with God (John 20:28). This is evidence enough that to call Jesus 'Lord' carried with it implications of deity, and this is certainly borne out in the other New Testament evidence.

In his first speech Peter declared that God had made Jesus 'Lord' (Acts 2:36). On numerous occasions in Acts Jesus is described as 'the Lord Jesus Christ' or as 'the Lord Jesus', which suggests that his lordship had become so universally acknowledged that it was natural to refer to him in this way. The epistles support the same view. But there are some passages, especially in Paul, which give specific teaching on the lordship of Christ. In 1 Corinthians 16:22 Paul ends his epistle with a prayer in an Aramaic form which means 'Our Lord, come.' In two passages he writes in a way which suggests that an early Christian confession took the form 'Jesus is Lord' (Rom. 10:9; 1 Cor. 12:3). There is no reason to suppose that such a formula represented the full creed, but it seems likely that acknowledgement of the lordship of Christ involved all the essential elements of basic Christian faith. This was more than a confession; it was a commitment. In yet another passage Paul asserts that a time will come when all will acknowledge Jesus as Lord (Phil. 2:11), although in this case a general acknowledgement of his supreme sovereignty is in mind. There is no doubt that the theme of lordship formed a part of Paul's declaration of the gospel (2 Cor. 4:5). The evidence suggests that when Paul thought of Jesus as Lord he meant it in a unique sense. The lordship was linked with the creatorship of all things (1 Cor. 8:6). In Paul's thinking, Jesus often performed the same functions as God. It is not unlikely, therefore, that, for Paul, the title 'Lord' carried much of its Old Testament meaning.

A few other New Testament references to the lordship of Christ confirm the point of view already made (compare for instance Heb. 8:8–12; 1 Pet. 3:15; Rev. 17:14; 19:16). The New Testament reaches its climax in the acclamation of Jesus as 'Lord of lords'. All the evidence shows, therefore, that a unique significance attached to the title of 'Lord' when applied to Christ. The title's significance is increased when it is linked with the conviction that Jesus is also Son of God.

Son of God   On many occasions Jesus spoke of God as 'My Father' in a way which suggests a unique relationship, and one which is to be distinguished from the idea of God as Father of all men. In John 20:17 this distinction is made explicit. When Peter confessed Jesus as Messiah, he linked with that title 'Son of the living God' (Matt. 16:16), which clearly shows the sense in which the messianic title was intended. At his trial Jesus tacitly admitted to the high priest that he was the Son of God (Matt. 26:63,64). In the Gospels he often spoke of himself as 'the Son' (Matt. 11:25–27; and especially in John's Gospel). We must enquire in what sense Jesus intended this relation to the Father to be understood. The Son was sent to do the will of the Father (John 3:34; 5:36,37; 11:42). He was never conscious of not doing that will. Indeed, his own will was in perfect harmony with the Father's. Bearing this in mind we shall note some of the more significant passages which show Jesus' awareness of his sonship.

At the baptism of Jesus a heavenly voice declared his sonship (Mark 1:11). At the temptation in the wilderness, it is clear that the tempter acknowledged the divine sonship of Jesus (Matt. 4:3,6). At the transfiguration, a second heavenly voice witnessed to the same truth (Mark 9:2–7). It is however to John's Gospel that we must turn to fill out some aspects of the special meaning which sonship had for Jesus. Several of those who met him recognised him as Son of God (compare John 1:34,49; 11:27). There are many instances where the Father's love for his Son is specifically mentioned by Jesus (John 3:35; 5:20; 17:24). These references show how important his position as Son was to him. Indeed they show that the relationship was based, not on an authority structure, but on love. At the same time Jesus shows his dependence on his Father (John 5:19ff; 14:31). One of his statements – 'the Father is greater than I' (John 14:28) – is somewhat baffling when set against the unity of Father and Son in John 10:30; 17:11. The former statement must be understood in the light of the incarnation and the latter in the light of the identity of purpose and character of Father and Son. Jesus reveals no awareness that as Son he is inferior to the Father, although clearly the incarnation placed certain limitations upon him.

A major implication of Jesus as Son of God is that he sees himself as the supreme revelation of the Father. He claims that the Son is the only one who has seen the Father (John 6:46). The words spoken by the Son are those of the Father (John 8:28; 15:15). Indeed he disclaims speaking any words of his own (John 12:49,50). Along with this is the remarkable statement that the Father 'has committed everything into the hands of the Son' (John 13:3), a fact which was much in the mind of Jesus as he faced the cross. He knew that death was not the end – he was returning to the Father (John 14:28). There can be no doubt that he was acutely conscious of his privileges and mission as Son of God, and it is not surprising that this title in reference to Jesus came to have such importance in the early church.

Admittedly there is not much stress on this title in Acts. The only references are in Acts 9:20; 13:33. But the epistles show how integral it was to the apostolic view of Jesus. Paul certainly had no doubt that Jesus was Son of God (Rom. 1:4). Several times he refers to Jesus in this way (for example, Rom. 1:9; Col. 1:13). Paul recognises that God was acting through his Son to redeem man (Gal. 4:4). Moreover, Paul anticipates a time when the Son, to whom all things are subjected, will subject himself to the Father (1 Cor. 15:28). For the apostle the fact that Jesus is Son of God was a most important feature of his theology.

Another New Testament writer who is strongly convinced that Jesus is Son of God is the writer to the Hebrews. Indeed, he introduces his readers to God's Son before he identifies him as Jesus. What he says about the Son in Hebrews 1:1–3 shows how exalted a view of Jesus he had. He is not only seen as the Creator and upholder of all things, but also as the reflector of God's glory and the bearer of his nature. He makes a great point of the superiority of the Son over the noblest of creatures, that is, the angels. He intends to present Jesus, being Son of God, as superior to all others. It is no wonder that as High Priest Jesus is seen to surpass the Aaronic priesthood. In fact the Son of God is superior to the law-giver Moses himself, who by comparison is no more than a servant (3:1–6).

We may conclude that Jesus was recognised as being in a unique sense Son of God. Although believers are also spoken of as 'sons' of God, this is in a derived sense compared with Jesus' sonship. The dual titles 'Lord' and 'Son of God' show that Jesus was more than just a perfect man. They imply that he was God as well as man, and this implication is confirmed when we consider the more specific New Testament evidence that Jesus was believed to be God.

Jesus, God as well as man
Although the definite evidence for Jesus being regarded as God is restricted to a few New Testament passages, these must be assessed against the background of the evidence already considered. We look first at John 1:1 which not only declares that the Word (clearly a name for Jesus, as 1:14 shows) was the agent of

creation, but also that he was with God and was God. There has been much discussion about why John introduces Jesus in this way. Some have suggested that 'Word' (Gk. *Logos*) would have been so familiar to Greek readers in the sense of an agent of God, that John wanted to tell them that no other *Logos* was effective except Jesus Christ. Others have wanted to interpret the Word in a more Jewish sense, that is, as Wisdom. They see some contact with Proverbs 8. Whatever the origin of the term, however, there can be no doubt that John sees the Word as God. It would not be correct to regard the last part of John 1:1 as meaning no more than that the Word was divine or that he was simply a god, as some have maintained. The word *God* is a predicate and the absence of the definite article is perfectly normal in that case. We must conclude, therefore, that John intends his readers to understand at once that the Jesus he is able to write about is none other than God in a human form.

This conviction is reinforced by John 1:18, where the most probable reading speaks of Jesus as 'the only begotten God', a remarkable affirmation. The Gospel ends with a confession by Thomas that the risen Jesus was 'My Lord and my God' (20:28). It is all the more significant that these evidences occur in the same Gospel, which, more than the others, presents Jesus as Son of God.

There is one statement in Paul's epistles which agrees completely with the evidence from John. In Romans 9:5 Paul includes a doxology which ascribes to Christ the clause: 'who is God over all, blessed for ever'. Many editors avoid such a direct affirmation as this by placing a full stop after Christ and treating the reference to God as a separate doxology, that is, 'God who is over all is blessed for ever'. But Paul's normal procedure is against this and it is most natural to suppose that he meant to identify Christ as God. In a passage in Titus 2:13 the apostle attributes both 'God' and 'Saviour' to Jesus Christ. A similar expression is found in 2 Peter 1:1.

Among the Old Testament quotations which the writer to the Hebrews includes in chapter 1, the most remarkable is the one from Psalm 45:6 ('Thy throne, O God, is for ever and ever'). These words are directly applied to Christ and the writer shows no hesitation in doing so. For him it was axiomatic that what was true of God was also true of Christ, and this implies that he saw no incongruity in calling Jesus 'God'.

The statements mentioned above are impressive, but there are other indirect considerations which fully support them. Doxologies, like those of Revelation 5:13 and 7:10 are ascribed to Christ.

Prayers are addressed to him (Acts 7:59,60; 1 Cor. 16:22). More-over, he does the works of God, as when he forgave sins (Matt. 9:2–6). The disciples offered worship to the risen Christ (Matt. 28:9). We may note further that Jesus is spoken of as Creator, as Saviour, and as Judge, all functions which are normally attributed to God. These developments are all the more remarkable in the light of the strong monotheism among the Jews, which would have raised difficulties for Jewish Christians when Jesus was thought of as God.

Conclusion

In the New Testament we have seen that Jesus is presented as perfect man as well as perfect God. This raises the problem how both could exist side by side, for it may be wondered how a perfect man could at the same time be God, or how God could ever in a real sense become man without impairing his deity. The New Testament neither discusses these questions nor shows any recognition of any problems associated with them. It was not until Greek thought influenced the theology of the church that attempts were made to explain the dual reality of Jesus as man and God. If we take the New Testament as our textbook on doctrine we are bound to exclude any view of Jesus which makes him to be anything less than a perfect man. His perfect humanity is essential for a right view of the incarnation. The Word became real flesh in order to identify with the world of men. It did not merely appear to have happened in this way. But at the same time the evidence shows that Jesus was more than a man.

Paul's assertion that God was in Christ reconciling the world (2 Cor. 5:19) shows something of the mystery of the incarnation. There may not be a wholly satisfactory explanation of the nature of Jesus Christ, but the New Testament presents its readers with One who is exalted at the right hand of God and is at the same time able to sympathise with man's infirmities. In face of this glorious mystery man can do no more than worship.

7

THE KINGDOM OF GOD

One of the most characteristic themes in the teaching of Jesus is the kingdom of God. So frequent is this idea that we must examine carefully what Jesus meant by it, and what it would have conveyed to his hearers. We need to find out to what extent the teaching of Jesus about the kingdom of God can be considered to be new, and how much it was simply reinforcing what was already known. The best way to approach such a quest is to preface our study of the New Testament evidence with a brief survey of the way the Old Testament and the intertestamental period looked at the idea of a kingdom of God.

The background

Old Testament   We have already seen that the idea that God is King is well-attested in both the Old Testament and the New Testament. God's kingship is often referred to (for example, Ps. 103:19; 145:11–13; Dan. 4:3). Moreover, he is not regarded merely as a temporary King but as an eternal King. Not only is he King over Israel (Exod. 15:18), but over all men (Jer. 46:18). It is because God is Creator that he has a claim to kingship (Ps. 95:3–5). From this it is a short step to the idea of a kingdom over which God is King. But this raises a problem. What precisely does the Old Testament foresee about the nature of the kingdom? It is not easy to answer this question, for the idea seems to have had several different components.

We note first of all that there are predictions which focus on the restoration of the kingdom of David (Isa. 9:6,7; 11:1–5; Jer. 23:5,6). As the Israelites recalled their history, the period when David was king stood out as the period of greatest glory, and it was natural that future hopes for Israel were linked with his name. After all, God had anointed him king. This did not mean that the kingship of God had lessened, for the earthly king was regarded as the representative of God. Nevertheless, among the prophets it was recognised that Israel as they knew it was far removed from the glorious kingdom for which all peoples looked, and this led to hopes of a future kingdom in which God would reign eternally through his representative. This constituted the messianic hope. Israel's enemies were to be defeated and Jerusalem was to become the centre of the world (Isa. 24:23; Obad. 21; Zech. 14:9–17). Although this hope of a future kingdom had strong religious foundations, it was basically political and material in its scope.

Between the Testaments   During the period between the Testaments, there was increasing speculation about the coming kingdom. The aim of the pious was to acknowledge God's present kingship by obedience to his will as seen in the law of Moses (the Torah). But hopes were still pinned to a future kingdom. The community at Qumran was in fact organised on the basis that this would soon take place. These Jews, who had withdrawn into the Judean desert, believed they themselves would form the core of the coming kingdom.

In addition to these hopes of a coming kingdom on earth, the belief developed that a heavenly kingdom would come subsequent to this messianic age. This was known as *the age to come* and was generally believed to follow the resurrection of the dead.

Yet another of the confused ideas about the kingdom came from the movement known as the Zealots, which was a political group with religious motives. They believed it was their task to overthrow the occupying powers in Palestine. Although they maintained that this could be accomplished only through violence, their declared aim was to acknowledge God alone as King.

It is against this background of various ideas that the teaching of Jesus about the kingdom of God must be examined. His teaching came to people who would in no sense be unfamiliar with the terms he used. It is the form of his teaching and the context in which he placed it that must engage our attention.

The meaning of the term 'kingdom of God' in the New Testament
In all but four of the references in Matthew's Gospel the kingdom is called the *kingdom of heaven*. In other Gospels it is uniformly called the *kingdom of God*. The former use is paralleled in rabbinical literature and seems to have been used out of reverence for the name of God, which was considered to be too sacred to mention. It is certain that no distinction may be drawn between the kingdom of God and the kingdom of heaven.

But what precisely does the word 'kingdom' mean in the teaching of Jesus? It is generally agreed that its major idea is to denote a reign. That is to say, it draws attention to the King and the way he rules rather than to an area or to a group of people over whom he rules. Nevertheless a king cannot reign unless he has a people and some defined group with conditions of membership. In view of what has already been said in the last section, it must be denied that Jesus had a political structure in mind. His teaching will make no sense unless it is seen in a spiritual framework.

The announcement of the kingdom
It is not without importance that even before Jesus taught anything about the kingdom, John the Baptist was announcing its near arrival. He may be regarded as the link between the old order and the new. He had something of the prophet about him. His rough clothing and life-style were reminiscent of Elijah. To the crowds who flocked to the desert to hear him, he announced the coming of the kingdom, but laid down the condition for entry as being repentance (Matt. 3:2). Linked with this announcement was the call to be baptised, which involved a definite response on the part of the hearers. John did not claim to inaugurate the kingdom, for this was to be done by the Coming One who would baptise 'with the Spirit and with fire' (Matt. 3:11). The reference to fire points to the judgement which would accompany the kingdom: John speaks graphically of the axe being laid at the root of the tree. Nevertheless, alongside this more severe side of the kingdom was the promise of the coming Spirit, an assurance that a new activity of God of a spiritual kind was about to take place.

The importance of John's announcement of the kingdom is seen in the fact that Jesus at the beginning of his ministry announces it in the same terms and with the same challenge to repentance (Matt. 4:17). The link between the old order and the new (the messianic age) is, therefore, plain.

The kingdom as a present reality

The fact that Jesus declared that the kingdom was near suggests that he considered that, in some sense, it was arriving in his ministry. In fact, it is not unreasonable to suppose that the activity of Jesus was a manifestation of the kingdom. This understanding of the situation is further supported by various statements which he made.

When Jesus declared to the disciples that the kingdom was in their midst (Luke 17:20, 21), he clearly did not mean that there would be a long delay. Moreover, he led them to think of the kingdom as spiritual. It was not the kind of thing you could point to and say, 'Look, here it is.'

Something of the powerful character of the kingdom is seen by the fact that Jesus was casting out demons by the Spirit. He claimed that this was evidence that the kingdom had come (Matt. 12:28). It looks as if the coming of the kingdom of God was linked with the overcoming of the kingdom of Satan. In himself Jesus demonstrated that Satan was already a defeated foe.

Again, when Jesus talked about John the Baptist, he declared that the kingdom of God had already suffered violence (Matt. 11:11,12; Luke 7:28). It is not clear what Jesus meant by this, but in all probability he meant that there was violent opposition to the coming of the kingdom. If we are right in supposing that Jesus was himself the kingdom, it is clear that his life and teaching roused much opposition. At least there is no doubt that the kingdom was seen as already present, for otherwise it could not be attacked.

One other saying confirms the same view. Jesus spoke of tax gatherers and harlots entering the kingdom before the religious leaders (Matt. 21:31). Since these social outcasts were responding to the teaching of Jesus, whereas the religious leaders were not, the kingdom is clearly connected with people's attitude to him in his present ministry.

If this were all the evidence about the kingdom it would be possible to say that when Jesus began his public ministry he inaugurated the kingdom. But in that case it would be necessary to discover what happened to the kingdom when Jesus died. When we turn to Acts we find that the early preachers proclaimed the kingdom just as Jesus had done (Acts 19:8; 20:25; 28:23, 31).

The kingdom is not as prominent in the epistles as in the Gospels, but is not absent. Paul gives both a negative and a positive idea of the kingdom. Entry is not conditional upon food taboos as some may have thought (Rom. 14:17), nor is the concept simply a matter of talk (1 Cor. 4:20). On the contrary, the kingdom consists of a worthy way of life, an acceptance of high moral demands. In this sense it is closely akin to a description of the new life in Christ.

In the book of Revelation, those who have been freed from sins through Christ are said to be a kingdom (Rev. 1:6), which comes close to identifying the kingdom with the church (compare also Rev. 1:9).

All the above evidence for the present nature of the kingdom must be balanced against the further evidence which sees it as something which Christians should look forward to in the future.

The kingdom as a future event

Although there is a sense in which the kingdom has already arrived, this would not be adequate unless it could in some ways be related to the future. We naturally want to know what the New Testament says about this aspect of the kingdom. It will then be necessary to discover how the present and future views are combined.

Jesus predicted a future coming of himself as Son of Man and this is linked with the idea of a kingdom (Matt. 25:31,34). In some of the beatitudes the promise of the kingdom is expressed as a future hope rather than as a present reality (Matt. 5:8). In the Lord's Prayer a request is included for the coming of the kingdom (Matt. 6:10). Jesus looks ahead to a coming banquet in which the patriarchs and God's sons from various parts of the world will participate (Matt. 8:11). The kingdom is where the righteous will 'shine as the sun' (Matt. 13:43), which clearly points to a future state.

The apostle Paul continues this future view of the kingdom in his references to the believer's inheritance (1 Cor. 6:9,10; 15:50). It is nevertheless significant that he uses this future hope of the kingdom as a basis for moral appeals (compare also Gal. 5:21; Eph. 5:5). In view of God's righteous judgement it is important to be made worthy of the kingdom (2 Thess. 1:5), but Paul never suggests that any man can make himself worthy.

Other New Testament writers bring out the same thought about a future kingdom. Hebrews 12:28 speaks of an 'unshakeable kingdom', James 2:5 of 'the kingdom prepared for those who love God', and 2 Peter 1:11 of an 'eternal kingdom'. But it is in Revelation that the focus falls most clearly on the coming kingdom. At the blowing of the seventh trumpet the kingdom of the world becomes 'the kingdom of our Lord and of his Christ' (Rev. 11:15),

63

an event which is celebrated in the worship passage in Revelation 12:10. In fact, the final intensification of evil will be expressed in a kind of counterfeit kingdom of antichrist.

The twofold aspect

We cannot avoid the conclusion that both the present and future views of the kingdom are equally strongly supported in the New Testament. There is no suggestion that the kingdom belongs exclusively to either. The present view has claimed the support of those who saw the gospel in terms of social involvement, whereas the future view has claimed the support of many who have no desire to become involved in the present. It is clearly necessary to find a way of combining the two views. Perhaps the best way of doing this is to merge the reign of God in the present into the final completion of that reign on the day when all will acknowledge the Lordship of Christ. Such a climax to the kingdom would also coincide with the handing over by Christ to God of all authority after the subduing of all enemies (1 Cor. 15:24–28).

Membership

If the kingdom idea is of such importance, especially in the teaching of Jesus, the conditions for participation in the kingdom are of paramount significance. There is no suggestion that any people can enter the kingdom irrespective of their attitude to its claims. There is a dividing line between those who respond and those who do not. How is the line drawn? It has already been shown that the kingdom assumes some moral claims, in that anyone unworthy is at once excluded. But more than this is involved. There is the question of commitment to Jesus himself, for Jesus expected his followers to be commited to the point of carrying their own crosses after him (Matt. 16:24) and to put him before family ties (Matt. 10:37). He even demanded a child-like spirit of trust in him from his disciples (Mark 10:13–16). With such stringent demands, one might wonder whether anyone would qualify. But Jesus did not expect people to qualify in their own strength. It is a matter of commitment, not of achievement. The whole kingdom teaching is not divorced from the constant emphasis on the need for faith. And this is especially noticeable in the epistles. Another requirement for entry to the kingdom, which it is even more evident that man cannot fulfil, is the demand for rebirth in John 3:3,5. This can be effected only by the Spirit. The kingdom consists, therefore, of regenerated people. In no clearer way could the impossibility of anyone doing anything to earn membership of the kingdom be emphasised.

Aspects of the kingdom

Although Jesus called the kingdom a 'mystery', its salient features may nevertheless be known. Looking at the parables is one way of discovering the ideas involved in Jesus' kingdom teaching. Admittedly Jesus knew that many would fail to grasp their real meaning, but he chose to teach in parables so that the discerning and those eager to learn would be able to receive the word. The group of parables in Matthew 13 gives a good example of his parabolic teaching about the kingdom.

Several of these parables contain the idea of *growth*. The parable of the sower shows that not all who hear about the kingdom will respond, although in many cases the seed will produce a good harvest. The parable of the tares also assumes a steady growth, but is intended to show the difficulty of defining the limits of the kingdom in the present age. In case people should find it hard to imagine that the kingdom of God could develop from such apparently small beginnings, Jesus told the parable of the mustard tree, growing amazingly quickly from a seed of insignificant size. All of these parables present an optimistic picture of growth in this age.

One aspect which is particularly important is the *value* of the kingdom. This value is so great that a man will give all he possesses to acquire it (as illustrated by the parables of the hidden treasure and the precious pearl). But this teaching is not meant to suggest that the kingdom may be obtained by material means, or that it even consists of something which can be acquired and owned. It is rather a group of people who will put as their first priority the service of God.

Certainly since the kingdom is already present in the ministry of Jesus it cannot be divorced from his mission of *salvation*. This is important if the connection between the death of Jesus and his kingdom teaching is to be understood. Those in the kingdom were those who had responded to the offer of forgiveness (Luke 5:20,21). Moreover, Jesus acknowledged that his exorcism of demon-possessed people was a demonstration of the kingdom's authority (Luke 11:20). This brings attention to the fact that the kingdom is a powerful agency for deliverance.

The relation between the kingdom and the church

We have already seen that there are certain aspects of the kingdom which are active in this age. This raises the question of the relation between the kingdom and the church. It must at once be noted that Jesus did not identify the two. He himself proclaimed the kingdom, and he taught his disciples to do the same. Nevertheless, it may be said that the church finds its basis in the kingdom. Peter is promised the keys of the kingdom in a passage which also mentions the church. It seems best to suppose that the kingdom is larger than the church, but every member of the true church is also a member of the kingdom. This leads to the idea that in the present age the kingdom (or rather kingly reign of Christ) is seen partially in the church.

The future of the kingdom

This present age, which may be called *the church age*, will have a conclusion at the future coming of Jesus. The conclusion of the church age will also mark the completion of the kingdom, and the handing over of the kingdom to God. Some maintain that at the coming of Jesus the kingdom will be established on earth for a thousand years, but it is not certain whether the New Testament requires this interpretation. Others maintain as strongly that Revelation 20, on which the period is based, should not be taken literally, but that the thousand years indicate 'the day of the Lord' (see further comments on this later).

8

THE ATONEMENT

A burning question which faces anyone who comes to the New Testament is the problem of explaining why Jesus died. This is even more acute when an examination of the New Testament shows that the man of Nazareth was also the Son of God. Since the gospel stories devote so much time to the record of the last week of Jesus' life, culminating in his death and resurrection (in Mark's Gospel, for instance, this amounts to about one third of the contents), it is evident that it plays a major part in the Gospel. Some explanation is demanded. Was Jesus simply a martyr for his cause? Was it all a mistake, a disillusionment? Or was there a purpose in it? Was it planned? Moreover, has the death of Christ any relevance at all for us today? These are the questions which the New Testament teaching on atonement sets out to answer.

Our examination of that teaching falls naturally into two parts: what Jesus himself thought about his own death and what the early Christians came to believe about the significance of that death. We shall find that Jesus gave little more than hints, but these are enough to form the basis of the later interpretation given by the apostles. The evidence shows that the latter did not build up a notion about the death of Jesus which was alien to what he intended. It is clear that at an early time there was the recognition that the death of Jesus was somehow related to sins, as Paul in 1 Corinthians 15:3 shows in a statement that he had received from others.

How did Jesus view his death?

We may at once dispense with the theory that Jesus did not expect to die in a violent way, for he three times predicted that it would happen. The first time was immediately before the transfiguration (Matt. 16:21) and this gave a jolt to all the disciples. Peter was probably expressing the consensus of opinion when he wanted at all costs to prevent what he considered to be a calamity (Matt. 16:22). But Jesus at once rebuked Peter in the strongest possible way. The details of Jesus' prediction were quite specific. He recognised that he must be killed, but that he would rise again on the third day. The twofold repetition of this kind of prediction reveals just how much importance Jesus attached to the significance of his death (Matt. 17:22, 23; 20:17–19). On the third occasion the manner of death is foreseen to be crucifixion. In no sense did his death on the cross take Jesus unawares or unprepared.

He had previously spoken of the 'bridegroom' being 'taken away' (Mark 2:18–20), which implied violent removal. He had also mentioned that the Son of Man would be three days and nights in the heart of the earth, as Jonah spent a similar period in the fish's belly (Matt. 12:40).

We need to enquire further into the interpretation Jesus gave of the significance of his death, and we shall do this under the following headings: the necessity for the death, its voluntary nature, its sacrificial aspects, its relation to man's sins, its fulfilment of Old Testament predictions, and its interpretation as a deliverance.

The necessity for the death

This has already been brought out in the predictions just mentioned, for Jesus had a sense of compulsion in going to Jerusalem where he knew he would die. This realisation that it was all part of a divine plan is also brought out particularly in John's Gospel, where Jesus several times mentioned the 'hour', which is the hour of his death. In the earlier part of the Gospel, he declared that his hour had not yet come (John 2:4; 7:6,8,30; 8:20), but by the time the narrative reaches the passion week he announced that his hour had now come (John 12:23). This remarkable sense of his impending destiny shows that in Jesus' mind his death was in no sense an accidental event. This sense of inevitable death is implicit in other statements. For instance, Jesus said that he must be 'lifted up' as Moses 'lifted up the serpent' (John 3:14), and he pointed out the necessity for a corn of wheat to fall into the ground and die if it was to produce more grain (John 12:24), a clear allusion to the necessity of his own death. Jesus' deep awareness that his death was planned plays an important part in enabling us to understand his mission. He was aware that the key event in his work was his death. We shall note below that the fact that God took the initiative is an indispensable part of the later Christian understanding of the cross.

The voluntary character of Jesus' death
The sense of inevitability brought out in the preceding section might lead to the idea that Jesus held a fatalistic view of his destiny, but nothing could be further from the truth. It is especially brought out in John's Gospel that the shepherd voluntarily 'lays down his life for the sheep' (John 10:11,15,17). Moreover, Jesus made it perfectly clear that no one was taking his life from him; he laid it down of his own accord (John 10:18). This double sense of God's plan and the deliberate choice of Jesus are both equally stressed in the Gospels, without any indication of tension between them. So totally dedicated was Jesus to the will of the Father that there could be no tension between what God had planned and what Jesus willed. This sense of commitment to God's will is vividly brought out in the prayer of Jesus in Gethsemane (Luke 22:42–44).

Its sacrificial aspects
By considering Jesus' concept of his death as a sacrifice, we are entering more specifically into the way in which he understood the meaning of his death. The words of John the Baptist, 'Behold, the Lamb of God, who takes away the sin of the world' (John 1:29), were accepted by Jesus and give a clear indication of his death in terms of sacrifice. The lamb was a familiar part of the Passover ritual and was sacrificed to atone for the sins of the people, and although John the Baptist makes no mention of the sacrificing of the Lamb, this is implicit in his statement.

When Jesus spoke of giving himself for the life of the world (John 6:51), the same idea of giving himself as a sacrifice for others is in mind. He identified himself as 'the heavenly bread' on which man could feed. The fact that in this context Jesus spoke of men eating his flesh and drinking his blood shows that death, not life, is in mind, since flesh and blood are separated. This saying from John's Gospel prepares us for an understanding of the words Jesus used at the Last Supper, which are not recorded in John but are in the other three Gospels. Since these words were given on the eve of the death of Jesus, they are of major importance in the interpretation of that death. We note first that the bread was broken as a symbol of the death of Jesus. There is certainly a sacrificial idea here, especially in the mention of the poured–out blood. This appears to be an allusion to the ratification of the old covenant in Exodus 24, which was accomplished by the sprinkling of the blood of sacrifice. Jesus refers to the blood of the new covenant and clearly associates it with his death. Moreover, because the blood is regarded as a basis for the forgiveness of sins (Matt. 26:28), there may well be an allusion to the suffering servant of Isaiah 53, who 'makes himself an offering for sin' (Isa. 53:10).

Although Jesus did not specifically command his disciples to repeat the Supper, it is evident that they recognised the need to do so, and thus the Supper itself became a constant reminder to them of the way Jesus meant them to understand his death. This is reinforced by the fact that in the form of wording which Paul received, the words, 'Do this in remembrance of me' (1 Cor. 11:24,25), are added to bring out the character of the Supper as a memorial. Some ancient authorities have similar words in Luke 22:20. It must be noted that all that Paul writes by way of interpretation of the death of Christ, should be seen in the light of the traditions he had received, which go back to the words of Jesus himself.

Its relation to man's sins

'The Lamb of God' takes away the sin of the world. The blood of the new covenant is shed for the forgiveness of sins. This idea of the close connection between the death of Christ and man's sins is of utmost importance for a right understanding of the meaning of that death. If Jesus died for sin, it must have been for other peoples' sins, since he himself was sinless. Something of the consciousness of the load of bearing the sins of others may account for the cry from the cross, 'My God, my God, why hast thou forsaken me?' (Matt. 27:46). Some notion of substitution, in which Christ consciously took the place of sinners, seems inescapable. Otherwise we would be obliged to treat the cry from the cross as a cry of disillusionment. But this latter view would conflict with the evidence which shows the death of Christ to be designed and voluntary.

Its fulfilment of Old Testament prophecy

We have already noted the parallel between the old and new covenants in the words given at the Last Supper. The parallel with the book of Exodus is strong. The same may be said about the connection between the institution of the Supper and Isaiah 53. There are many indications in the Acts and New Testament epistles that the early Christians recognised how significant Isaiah 53 was for an understanding of Jesus' mission (compare for instance Acts 8 and 1 Pet. 2:22–24). There is no reason to suppose that Jesus was not himself conscious of fulfilling the role of the suffering servant. Undoubtedly the early Christians appealed constantly to the Old Testament in their exposition of the significance of Jesus, as the many citations from the Old Testament in the New Testament show.

The death of Christ as a deliverance
The clearest passage which gives an understanding of the purpose of his death in the mind of Jesus is Mark 10:45 (paralleled in Matt. 20:28). Jesus, as Son of Man, sees himself as 'a ransom for many'. This word *ransom* is connected with the price paid for the freeing of slaves. When the ransom had been paid the slave at once became a free man. Nothing is said about the one to whom the ransom would be paid, but the ransom consisted of the life of the Son of Man given for others. Jesus here seems to be seeing man in bondage and in need of deliverance. This theme is further developed in the epistles under the idea of redemption.

Under this same consideration we may include the statements of Jesus which view his coming death in terms of victory. He announced that the ruler of this world was to be cast out (John 12:31). He spoke of his death in terms of being lifted up, which could refer to death by crucifixion, but could also be a reference to his coming exaltation. Jesus spoke in the same context of his glorification. Moreover, in John's Gospel the concluding word from the cross was 'It is finished' (John 19:30), which is not a cry of defeat but of victory.

We may conclude, therefore, that for Jesus the cross was no accident. It was a part of God's plan in sending him to deliver men from their present bondage. For Jesus it was also the path to his glorification and exaltation.

How did the early Christians view the death of Jesus?
As soon as we pass from the Gospels to the book of Acts we find that the death and resurrection of Jesus figure prominently in the preaching of the apostles. There is no doubt that the resurrection made all the difference to the disciples' attitude towards the death of Jesus. Jesus was seen as the conqueror of death. Never is the crucifixion mentioned without the accompanying resurrection. It

is important nonetheless to discuss what they made of the death in the light of the resurrection.

In the speech of Peter on the day of Pentecost he made the astonishing statement that the crucifixion was part of the deliberate plan of God, although he did not exempt from responsibility the men who had killed Jesus (Acts 2:23). This at once introduces a paradox, but the early Christians were not troubled by it. They knew that Jesus had willingly accepted death and that he himself had seen it as part of God's plan. But they did not forget that wicked men had actually done the deed.

The early apostles were also deeply convinced that what had happened to Jesus had been foretold in scripture (Acts 3:18). There is every possibility that this conviction was based on the exposition by the risen Christ from the scriptures which pointed to a suffering Messiah (Luke 24:25,26, 44). We note that in two passages in the Acts speeches Jesus is described as a servant (Acts 3:13,26; 4:27,30), and it is natural to suppose that on both occasions Peter had in mind the identification of Jesus with the suffering servant of Isaiah. This strong link between Christ and the Old Testament helps us to understand that, in their attempts to interpret the death of Christ, the apostles were not starting from scratch. For those who could read the clear predictions of God in scripture, what happened to Jesus was not unexpected.

The first preachers had no hesitation in proclaiming forgiveness of sins on the grounds of the work of Christ and following upon the repentance and faith of the sinner (Acts 2:38; 3:19; 5:31; 10:43; 13:38). In one of Paul's speeches the apostle speaks in terms of Christ having 'obtained' his church through his own blood (Acts 20:28). There is, therefore, throughout the record of the early preachers, a tremendous sense of the importance of the death of Christ for the very existence of the Christian church.

We must not be unduly surprised that the book of Acts contains so little interpretation of the cross. It was sufficient in addresses to non-Christian audiences to call on men to repent and to accept forgiveness. It was left to the more reflective letters to supply some richer metaphors to throw light on the mystery of Christ's death. We shall deal with these under various aspects.

When considering Paul's evidence it is important to note that he was building on earlier interpretations. He shows clearly in 1 Corinthians 15:3,4 that he had 'received' that Christ died for our sins according to the scriptures, and that he was buried and rose again on the third day. The statement that Christ died for our sins gives no indication of how this could have happened, or how it could be explained. This did not deter Paul from using a wide variety of concepts to develop the ideas which were inherent in the 1 Corinthians statement. It should also be noted that when the apostle refers to the words of institution of the Last Supper he maintains that he received this 'from the Lord'. Since this is a key passage in Paul's understanding of the death of Christ, it is clear that he is conscious that his interpretation is based on revelation and not on his own wisdom. Although none of the other New Testament writers brings this out so clearly, it is evident from an examination of their writings that there was a general agreement about the central significance of the death of Christ for the Christian faith.

Jesus as a sacrifice

It is not altogether surprising that Christians began to think of the way Jesus died in terms of sacrifice. The Jews would especially be conscious of the significance of animal sacrifices in man's approach to God. But the Christian Jew would want to re–interpret the sacrificial idea in terms of the death of Christ and this is precisely what Paul does. He calls Christ 'our paschal lamb' (1 Cor. 5:7), which shows him transferring the ideas connected with the Passover to Christ in a meaningful way. This comes out in the reference to the blood of the new covenant (1 Cor. 11:25), for, when the old covenant was ratified, the book of the covenant and the worshippers were sprinkled with the blood of sacrifice (Exod. 24). We have already noted that some analogy with this is seen in the words of institution. It was intended that as often as the Last Supper was to be observed Christ's sacrificial act should be recognised.

There are many instances in the New Testament where the word 'blood' is used to refer to the death of Christ (compare Rom. 3:25; 5:9). One advantage of this term is that it includes the idea of life as well as death, although its main emphasis is on the death. It is particularly in the letter to the Hebrews that we find the real significance of the blood of Christ. The weakness of the old system of sacrifices is brought out in connection with the exposition of the inadequacy of the priesthood of Aaron. The blood of animals could never take away sins (Heb. 10:4), which means that a more adequate type of offering had to be provided and this is seen in the offering of Christ. Indeed, the most important difference between the Levitical sacrifices and the death of Christ is the fact that Christ offered himself, that his offering was complete (once for all), and that the offering was made through the eternal Spirit

(Heb. 9:14). There was a voluntary character about the death of Christ which was entirely absent from the Old Testament sacrifices. Another point that should be noted is that the book of Hebrews speaks of a heavenly 'holy of holies' into which Christ entered (Heb. 9:7–14), and this again contrasts the sacrifice of Christ with all preceding sacrifices.

There are several passages in 1 Peter where sacrificial language is used (1 Pet. 1:2; 1:18,19; 2:22–24; 3:18). Particularly in 1 Peter 2:22–24 the language is reminiscent of Isaiah 53. The idea of blood having some kind of cleansing effect is also brought out in 1 John 1:7, again in relation to the blood of Christ. John affirms that the sinless One could take away sin, although he does not say how (1 John 3:5). The voluntary character of the death of Christ is, however, brought out in 1 John 3:16.

We cannot leave the theme of Christ's death as a sacrifice without mention of the Lamb in the book of Revelation. Although the whole theme of the book is to portray the Lamb as victorious over all his enemies, yet the sacrificial aspect is nonetheless present in that the Lamb is a slain Lamb, who is very much alive (Rev. 5:6). Even the warrior Christ who comes at the end of the age is the same person as the Lamb (Rev. 19), and this book vividly brings before the reader the connection between the two ideas. Those who are seen as the people of God are those whose robes are washed in the blood of the Lamb (Rev. 7:14).

Jesus as a substitute
We need to investigate whether there is evidence that the New Testament writers thought that in his death Jesus did something in the place of others. To put it another way, did Jesus in any sense carry the punishment which should have been borne by sinful men? The idea that a just man died for the unjust does not at first appeal to us as morally right. And yet such a statement is specifically made in 1 Peter 3:18. There is no suggestion that the idea is unacceptable. Peter is writing about suffering and he knows that many Christians have suffered wrongfully. He sees the sufferings of Christ as an example (1 Peter 2:21), but he does not leave it there. He sees a distinction between Christians suffering wrongfully and Christ suffering for the unrighteous, yet without sin.

This idea is expressed as forcefully by Paul in 2 Corinthians 5:21, when he states that God made Christ to 'be sin' for us. In view of his deep conviction about the sinlessness of Christ, Paul cannot have had in mind anything less than the idea that in some way our sin was transferred to Jesus. Something of the same concept is found in Galatians 3:13, where the apostle speaks of Christ becoming a curse for us.

On many occasions Paul speaks of Christ doing things 'for' men. His body was broken 'for you' (1 Cor. 11:24). God gave his Son 'for us all' (Rom. 8:32). Christ died 'for all' (2 Cor. 5:15). These examples show that Paul thought of Christ's death as being on man's behalf. He does not, however, explain *how* this can take place. He merely affirms it as a fact. Certainly in 1 Timothy 2:6 he takes up the idea of Christ being a ransom for us, which echoes the teaching of Jesus (Mark 10:45) and involves the same thought of Jesus having done something in our stead.

Jesus as a propitiation

Many would prefer to avoid the use of this term because it conjures up the wrong idea. It originally meant some kind of offering which would placate an angry god. But this pagan use of the term is far removed from its use in the New Testament. In his Roman letter Paul uses the word when he says that God put forward Christ as a propitiation (RSV has 'expiation') by his blood (Rom. 3:25). Clearly he is not thinking in terms of placating anger, for it is God himself who provides the propitiation. Yet he must mean that God did something in Christ, directly connected with his death, which enables the believer to stand in a right relationship with God. We can understand this only if we take into account what Paul also says about the wrath of God (compare Rom. 1:18). There is no sense in which the apostle thinks of God as venting his anger against men. For him the wrath of God is the reaction of holiness to all that is unholy. For God to receive man into fellowship there had to be some way of removing the obstacle, that is, the enmity which exists between sinful man and a holy God (compare Rom. 5:6–11).

A somewhat similar statement is found in Hebrews 2:17, where our High Priest is said to make expiation for our sins, that is, he makes amends for our sins. It will be noted that in this case the emphasis falls on *sins* rather than on relationship. The same is true of 1 John 2:2, where Jesus Christ the righteous is said to be the expiation for our sins and for the sins of the whole world.

Again we must conclude that the New Testament writers viewed the death of Christ as something which he endured to enable man to approach a holy God, and without which such an approach would not be possible.

Jesus as a redeemer

The idea of his death as a means of deliverance has been noted in the teaching of Jesus, and this idea is further developed in Paul's doctrine of redemption. The word for ransom has a direct relation to the word Paul uses for redemption. We shall note the way in which the apostle several times introduces this theme.

The passage about propitiation in Romans (Rom. 3:25) considered in our last section is important for our present theme, for Paul maintains in the same context that it is through the redemption which is in Christ Jesus that we are justified by the grace of God. What precisely does he mean? He seems to be pointing to the cost of our salvation, which is nothing less than the blood of Christ. This idea of costs fits in well with the freedom from slavery idea in the ransom passage in Mark 10:45.

There is a close connection between ransom and forgiveness in Ephesians 1:7, again with an emphasis on the blood of Christ as the cost of the operation. It is noticeable also that Paul makes clear in this passage that the act of redemption has already taken place. Christians are already delivered from the bondage of sin. In one passage (1 Cor. 1:30) Paul actually calls Jesus 'our redemption'.

In addition to the use of the word 'redemption' Paul follows up the idea of cost by claiming that Christians are not their own, but are 'bought with a price' (1 Cor. 6:19,20). This is a development of the slavery imagery, for those who are freed from the bondage of sin do not become free men in the sense of being able to live wholly independent lives. For Paul, deliverance from sin also involves deliverance to a new service. He speaks of himself as a servant (or bond-slave) of Jesus Christ (Rom. 1:1). In Galatians 3:13 Christ is said to have redeemed us 'from the curse of the law', which must mean that he has released us from the adverse consequences of our having broken the law.

In some other parts of the New Testament the redemption theme is clearly brought out. In 1 Peter 1:18,19 we find the statement that we are not ransomed by corruptible things such as money, but by the precious blood of Christ. Again the greatness of the cost is in mind. The same theme forms a major anthem in the scene of heavenly worship in Revelation 5:9,10, and again reference is made to the blood of Christ. The many glimpses of the saints in this book remind us that they are a people who have been delivered from the effects of the evil environment around them.

There is no doubt that this theme of redemption is an important aspect of the New Testament teaching about the work of Christ and the significance of the cross. It must be made clear, however, that nowhere in the New Testament is there any discussion of the question to whom the ransom is paid. The writers are content to use the analogy of the freeing of slaves to draw attention to the cost, in order to emphasise the obligation to service which falls to those redeemed. It cannot be too strongly stressed that redemption is not only *from* sin, but also *to* a higher form of service to God.

Jesus as High Priest

A whole New Testament book (Hebrews) is devoted to this theme, but it does not figure prominently elsewhere. It is remarkable because it presents Jesus not only in sacrificial terms as the only adequate offering, but also as the Priest who makes the offering. We may briefly summarise the teaching of Hebrews on the High Priest theme as follows.

Readers of the Old Testament would be familiar with the provision for ancient Israel of a priestly system, which was headed up by the high priest as the representative of the people before God. The main weakness of the Aaronic priesthood was that the priests were themselves sinful men and needed to bring offerings for themselves as well as for the people (Heb. 5:3). In contrast, Jesus as High Priest has no need to offer for himself, because he is sinless (Heb. 7:26). In any case he does not offer daily sacrifices as the Aaronic priests had to do, because his death is regarded as a once–for–all act, which never needs to be repeated.

The writer to the Hebrews develops the theme of the priesthood of the order of Melchizedek (especially in Heb. 7). This priesthood is superior to Aaron's order for several reasons. Melchizedek was a priest king, whereas Aaron was not. Moreover, his priesthood is reckoned to be eternal, which means that it was not dependent, as Aaron's was, on a line of succession. This was a fitting picture for the totally unique Priesthood of Christ. It is noticeable also that our High Priest, unlike any of Aaron's line, made the offering of himself. There was no precedent for this. One feature in which Jesus excels is his ability to plead for his people. He has deep sympathy for them (Heb. 2:17,18; 4:15; 7:25). Moreover, Jesus as High Priest holds an exalted position since he is seated on the right hand of the throne of God (Heb. 1:3; 8:1; 12:2).

Closely linked with this theme is the idea of Jesus as the mediator of the new covenant (Gal. 3:19,20; 1 Tim 2:5,6). The essential task of the mediator is to act as a go-between in man's relationship with God.

Jesus as the reconciler

Because sin has created a barrier between man and God, it is essential for some method of reconciliation to be found. This is another theme to which Paul gives particular attention. He has two classic passages. In Romans 5:8–11, he shows how God set out to reconcile man, when man was still an enemy. Hostility existed between man and God, and no fellowship was possible unless the barrier was removed. That barrier, in Paul's view, is connected with God's wrath, and the method of reconciliation is said to be the death of his Son. Here, in a remarkable way, God's wrath and love are combined.

It is no wonder that, when Paul wants to describe his own ministry, he thinks of it as a 'ministry of reconciliation' (2 Cor. 5:18). He sees himself as an ambassador for God, beseeching people to be reconciled because God has already in Christ reconciled us to himself. This means that God will no longer count men's trespasses to be a barrier to their coming to him. This was the glorious message which Paul had to proclaim. It summed up for him the whole gospel. It was nevertheless based on the mystery that Christ was made 'sin' for us (2 Cor. 5:21).

Jesus as the justifier

Paul's great doctrine of justification by faith must be regarded as another aspect of his teaching about the cross. This theme is expounded in Romans and Galatians. The main points to note are the impossibility of man doing anything to earn his salvation, the fact that through the death of Christ there is now no condemnation for the people of God, and the fact that through faith alone the justifying act of God can become a reality.

Since the root idea of justification is to declare someone righteous, it cannot be considered apart from the New Testament idea of judgement, which in turn is bound up with the concept of righteousness. It is assumed without discussion that when God judges he judges in a just way. When Paul speaks of 'the righteousness of God' he means it to be understood in the sense that God acts in a righteous way, because in fact he is holy. Such righteousness has now been revealed in the good news about the death of Jesus Christ (Rom. 1:17). This is the starting point for Paul's discussion of justification by faith. According to Romans 3:26, it is *because* God is righteous that he justifies *sinful* men.

Paul's whole argument is linked with his idea of the law of God, according to which man in his sin must be pronounced guilty. There have been some attempts to get away from this legal view by alleging that it evokes an unreal situation, in which a man who is acquitted still acts as if he were guilty. But this is to misunderstand Paul's doctrine. He makes no secret of the fact that, apart from God's justifying act, there would be no possibility of pardon. It is impossible to say why God can justify the sinner on the grounds of the death of Christ, but Paul does not hesitate to affirm that this is precisely what God does. In this way God deals with man's guilt and at the same time is seen to be acting righteously.

Without doubt the most important aspect of Paul's doctrine of justification is that it is effected by God. It does not depend on man's achievement. It requires only an act of faith. This doctrine does away with a system of merit and places all men on an equality before God.

Conclusion

We have found a rich variety in the New Testament interpretation of the death of Christ. In no sense can that death on a cross be regarded as an accident. It was not only planned by God, but became the sole ground on which man might approach God. As a result of it all barriers are swept away which previously prevented man's communion with God. What seemed at first to be a historical disaster has come to be acknowledged as the central act of God in saving mankind. No presentation of the Christian faith which leaves out the saving significance of the cross can be claimed to be New Testament faith. The gospel consists in the proclamation of what God in Christ has already done, on the strength of which man is called on to repent and believe.

9

THE
HOLY SPIRIT

One of the most important themes in the New Testament is the teaching about the Holy Spirit, because the activity of the Spirit is so vital to the Christian life. Much confusion about the Spirit springs from an inadequate understanding of the evidence. It is necessary, therefore, to make some kind of survey of the rich variety of activities which are attributed to the Spirit in the New Testament. Our study will be split into two main sections. We shall look at the Gospels to discover the teaching about the Spirit before the day of Pentecost, and at the rest of the New Testament for the post-Pentecost experience and teaching.

The Spirit of God in the life of Jesus
When God sent his Son into the world he chose to do so by miraculous means. It was through a virgin that Jesus was born, but the Gospel writers explain this as being brought about by the Holy Spirit (Matt. 1:18; Luke 1:35). Our introduction to the Spirit in the New Testament is dramatic and mysterious. Never before has a woman conceived through the intervention of the Spirit, and never since has it happened. The Spirit is therefore engaged in a miracle as Jesus became man. It is not surprising that a human life begun in such a manner should be directed throughout by the same Spirit and this is the impression conveyed by the Gospels. While Jesus was yet an infant the Spirit led Simeon to predict that

he would become a 'light' for the Gentiles and a 'glory' for God's people Israel (Luke 2:25–35). The Spirit therefore portrays Jesus in no narrow nationalistic terms, but as a universal Saviour. The Spirit also predicts that anguish would come to the soul of Mary, which links the birth of Jesus at once with his death.

John the Baptist, when he predicted the mission of Jesus, declared that he would baptise 'with the Holy Spirit and with fire' (Luke 3:15–16). This is a remarkable early indication that the Spirit would come to the people of God through Jesus, a foreshadowing of the events at Pentecost. The link of the Spirit with fire is a reminder that his work is purifying. The coming of the Spirit would involve a challenging, and even disturbing, experience.

At the commencement of the public ministry of Jesus, two important events are attributed to the Spirit, showing the vital part which the Spirit played in the launching of that ministry. When Jesus came to John the Baptist to be baptised, the Spirit descended upon him and a heavenly voice witnessed that Jesus was the beloved Son (Matt. 3:16,17; Mark 1:10,11; Luke 3:22). The two features are inseparable. The Spirit's coming on Jesus was as much a divine seal on his work as the heavenly voice. The descent was seen to be in the form of a dove, which may symbolise gentleness or peace, both characteristic of the Spirit. It is not surprising that almost immediately after this we are informed that the Spirit led (Mark says 'drove') Jesus into the wilderness to be tempted (Mark 1:12; Matt. 4:1; Luke 4:1). The Spirit was clearly superintending the preparation of Jesus for his mission. The specific temptations which Matthew and Luke record were an essential part of that preparation. There is no suggestion that the temptations were in any sense accidental. They came to Jesus because of the person he was and because of the special task he had come to perform. We may say that the Holy Spirit was the inaugurator of the public ministry of Jesus.

Having thus set the scene, the Spirit does not figure prominently in the remainder of the public ministry of Jesus according to the accounts of the evangelists. But in two activities the Spirit's participation is noted. It was by the Spirit that Jesus cast out evil spirits. Matthew notes that he cast out demons by 'the Spirit of God' (Matt. 12:28), although Luke has 'the finger of God' (Luke 11:20). This at once distinguishes the exorcisms of Jesus from the magical incantations used by many of the pagan exorcists. Moreover, the Spirit shows through these exorcisms the complete victory of Jesus over the forces of darkness. It is a significant reminder that the Holy Spirit is more powerful than the spirits of evil.

In his first public address Jesus, according to Luke 4:16–21, claimed that the promise of Isaiah 61:1,2 was fulfilled in himself. This passage spoke of the Spirit, and Jesus claimed its fulfilment that day in the synagogue at Nazareth. Again, the Spirit's action is seen to permeate the teaching ministry, one of the most important aspects of his public life. This ties up with Jesus' promise that the Spirit would bring to the disciples' memory all that he had taught them (John 14:26).

The Spirit of God in the teaching of Jesus

For the sake of clarity we will arrange the teaching under headings which will bring out the various characteristics of the Spirit.

The Spirit brings life

A Jewish teacher like Nicodemus found great difficulty in understanding the words of Jesus about being 'born of the Spirit' (John 3:5). Nevertheless, Jesus clearly meant that the Spirit of God could so work on a person that he would become a new creature. Nicodemus could think only of natural birth, but Jesus was concerned with spiritual realities. This passage in John 3 shows that new life in Christ can come only through the Spirit; it cannot happen simply through the will of man. The analogy of Jesus about the wind (John 3:8) was intended to underline the sovereign activity of the Spirit. The new birth is a mystery, but is an essential experience for those who are to have any real understanding of the Spirit of God. Apart from his activity, no one could become a child of God. If John 6:63 refers to the Holy Spirit, this brings further support to the theme that it is the Spirit who gives life. Moreover, the spiritual character of that life is seen to be opposite to a life lived 'according to the flesh', that is, dominated by selfish motives and material goals. This idea of a clash between the flesh and the Spirit will be mentioned again when Paul's teaching is considered.

The Spirit is promised

The promise of the Spirit is brought out in various ways. In Luke's account of the appearances of the risen Christ, the promise is given to the disciples that they would be clothed with power (Luke 24:49) if they waited in the city. This is a clear forward reference to the coming of the Spirit at Pentecost. The book of Acts bears out this powerful aspect of the work of the Spirit, not only in the events at Pentecost, but also in the developing work of the Christian church.

The promise of the Spirit given by Jesus is recorded in John's Gospel. When Jesus spoke of 'rivers of living waters', John comments that he was referring to the Spirit, whom believers would receive after Jesus was glorified (John 7:38,39). This link between living waters and the Spirit is interesting because of the idea of an overflow, showing that possession of the Spirit is to be shared.

Another very significant statement about the gift of the Spirit stresses its unlimited nature. God never stints when he gives. He never gives by measure (John 3:34). It is clearly God's will that all who proclaim the words of God should have the unlimited assistance of the Holy Spirit. This was not only seen in the preaching of Jesus, but also in the preaching of the apostles, as the book of Acts shows.

The Spirit as an aid to worship

During the conversation between Jesus and the woman of Samaria, the question of true worship was raised, and Jesus pointed out that God must be worshipped in spirit and in truth (John 4:23). Although this is not a direct reference to the Holy Spirit, it is almost certainly intended to show that true worship must be Spirit-led. This is not surprising in view of the fact that God is Spirit (John 4:24).

We may note in this connection that the baptismal formula in Matthew 28:19 includes a reference to the Spirit, which shows the importance of the Spirit's work in the special activities of the church.

The Spirit as the inspirer of scripture

It is of particular interest to note that Jesus attributes Psalm 110 to David, inspired by the Spirit (Mark 12:36). This reflects an acceptance of the full inspiration of scripture and accounts for the high value which Jesus placed on the testimony of the Old Testament. This view of inspiration is found similarly in the epistles and may be said to be the basic view of the early Christian church. It is of great importance in establishing the divine origin of the Old Testament scriptures. The fact that the Spirit inspired the text undergirds the authority which the Old Testament everywhere has in the New Testament.

The Spirit and the unforgivable sin

One of the most difficult sayings of Jesus is the one in which he draws a distinction between blasphemy against himself as Son of Man and blasphemy against the Holy Spirit (Mark 3:29; Matt.

12:31; Luke 12:10). The best understanding of this saying is to regard blasphemy against the Holy Spirit as a state of mind so hardened against the revelation of God that repentance becomes impossible. This saying again highlights the important part played by the Spirit of God in the mission of Jesus.

The Spirit as the Paraclete

The most informative collection of sayings about the Spirit occurs in John's Gospel in the block of teaching given by Jesus on the eve of the passion. There are five such sayings in which the Spirit is called 'the Paraclete' or 'the Spirit of truth' (or both). These are John 14:15–17; 14:25,26; 15:26,27; 16:5–11; 16:12–15. They contain some important features which may be summarised as follows.

The Spirit as a person   This characteristic is seen from the functions which the Spirit performs, from the titles applied to him and from the use of the masculine rather than the neuter pronoun in John 16:13. The first point depends on the fact that the Spirit's activities such as bearing witness or giving guidance would make no sense if the Spirit were an impersonal force. Moreover, a title like 'Paraclete', which in essence means one called alongside to help, may be rendered 'Counsellor', 'Helper', 'Advocate'. Whatever the precise meaning, the personal element is undeniable.

This aspect of the Spirit is of special importance for the New Testament teaching on the Trinity, for the personal nature of the Spirit is a prior assumption to any idea of a trinity of persons. We might add to this the statement in John 15:26 that the Spirit proceeds 'from the Father', which presupposes that the Spirit shares the same nature as the Father.

The Spirit as dwelling in believers   It is not easy to switch from the idea of the Spirit as a person to consider his indwelling of Christians, but this latter feature is a key theme in Paul's teaching about the Spirit. According to John 14:17, it is the indwelling Spirit who at once distinguishes the people of God from the people of the world. Something of the meaning of this indwelling is given in John 14:16, where the Spirit is called 'another Counsellor', which shows that the Spirit performs precisely the same function as Jesus himself had done among them. This suggests that the Spirit dwelling within the believer has the same meaning as Christ dwelling in the believer. There is much in Jesus' teaching in this context about abiding in Christ and Christ abiding in us, which links up with the indwelling presence of the Spirit.

The Spirit as the glorifier of Christ   There is no doubt that the major function of the Spirit is to witness to, and therefore to glorify, Christ (John 16:13,14). The Spirit does not draw attention to himself, neither does he speak on his own authority. This fact should provide a valuable test for the validity of claims which appeal to the activity of the Spirit. Movements which focus on the Spirit's working must guard against the danger of exalting the Spirit at the expense of Christ.

The Spirit's task is to witness to Christ and by virtue of this it is the Spirit who enables believers to witness to Christ (John 15:26,27). There is no possibility of the church spreading apart from the activity of the Spirit. The book of Acts bears strong witness to this.

The Spirit as an aid to memory   For the future of the church it was essential that reliable records should be preserved of the teaching of Jesus and this could not be left to the unreliable memories of men. It is for this reason that Jesus promised the aid of the Spirit for the process of recall (John 14:26). This would be sufficient to guarantee the truth. Indeed, this promise is an essential link in the establishing of the New Testament canon.

The Spirit as a guide   Jesus never intended that his people should be left without reliable guidance. The Spirit of God was to be the guide to truth (John 16:13), which means to say that he would be the interpreter. In the development of Christian doctrine this would be another indisputable feature, if the truth was to be preserved. A special aspect of this promise is that it relates to the future.

The Spirit in the world   Not only is the Spirit promised to believers, but he is also the one who would convict the world of sin (John 16:8–11). What is meant by sin in this context is a refusal to believe in Jesus, and the passage suggests that it is only by the Spirit that the world can recognise the true nature of unbelief. The convicting activity of the Spirit was to play a dominant role in the missionary outreach of the church. In no clearer way could Jesus show the overruling influence of the Spirit in the life of the church.

The Spirit as a gift   Jesus never suggested that there was any way in which people could work to secure the Spirit. It is the Father who gives the Spirit in response to the prayer of Jesus (John 14:16). It is clear, moreover, that the many promises about the

Spirit are relevant only to those who believe in Jesus. The activity of the Spirit is seen, therefore, to be a provision of God's grace. When Jesus appeared to the disciples in the upper room after his resurrection, he breathed on them and promised that they would receive the Spirit (John 20:22). In this latter instance the disciples received authority to forgive or retain sins, which shows that the gift of the Spirit brought with it great responsibilities.

We may conclude this brief survey of the teaching about the Holy Spirit in John's Gospel by noting its wide scope and many-sided character. From it we may recognise that much of the teaching in the epistles on the subject can claim a direct link with the teaching of Jesus. Indeed, it will be seen from the following survey of evidence that there is a remarkable oneness in the New Testament teaching. No true understanding of the total New Testament teaching is possible without giving considerable weight to the part played by the Holy Spirit.

The Spirit in the Acts

Whereas in John's Gospel the emphasis falls on predictions about the Spirit, in Acts we meet with the activity of the Spirit in fulfilment of the predictions. Our first consideration will be the record of Pentecost in Acts 2. Luke begins his book with a few references to the Spirit before the account of Pentecost. He mentions that Jesus gave commandments through the Spirit (Acts 1:2), that John the Baptist had predicted that Jesus would baptise with the Spirit (1:5), that the risen Jesus had promised the disciples power through the Spirit (1:8) and that the Spirit had inspired David in the writing of Psalms 69 and 109, which he quotes. All of these points receive further elucidation in the body of the book.

No one would dispute the importance of the day of Pentecost in the development of the Christian church. It was that event which transformed the disciples into a group of people who were able to turn the world 'upside down'. We note first that the coming of the Spirit was accompanied by wind and fire, symbolic of the power and cleansing quality of the Spirit's activities. It is significant that such signs of the coming were not repeated elsewhere and this must be explained by the uniqueness of the occasion.

At Pentecost there was no believer who did not receive the Spirit. Luke states that they were all filled with the Spirit (Acts 2:4). No distinctions were made and it is clear that the fullness of the Spirit was intended to be the experience of the whole community. A great deal of discussion has surrounded the gift of tongues received at Pentecost, particularly in its relationship to the gift of tongues mentioned by Paul in 1 Corinthians. It is evident from Acts 2 that people were speaking in known languages. No interpretation was necessary. This at once distinguishes the gift from the Corinthians' tongues. It is noticeable also that the coming of the Spirit was recognised as a direct fulfilment of Old Testament prophecy.

In the course of the Acts history it becomes clear that the Spirit played a dominant role. The Spirit was not only responsible for the initial thrust of evangelism, but was the source and inspiration of the ongoing life of the church. The Spirit brought the Christians together in close bonds of fellowship (Acts 2:41–47; 4:32–35). The Spirit also acted as judge where any act threatened to undermine that fellowship, as in the case of Ananias and Sapphira (Acts 5:3,4). Those called to exercise administrative functions were expected to be men of the Spirit (Acts 6:3). It was through the powerful enabling of the Spirit that Stephen was able to defend his faith among the Hellenists. Further, the Spirit exercised the gift of prophecy in the case of Agabus (Acts 11:28; 21:10–14).

In the extension of the church beyond the Jewish area, the Spirit played an important part, as in the case of the converts at Samaria (Acts 8:17) and the case of Cornelius and his household (Acts 10:44). The Spirit's direction is seen in the details of Philip's meeting with the Ethiopian (Acts 8:29,39) and on numerous occasions affecting the movements of the apostle Paul (compare Acts 13:1–4; 13:9; 13:52; 16:6,7). The Spirit who had been active in Paul's conversion also overruled his mission. Indeed it could be said that the book of Acts could appropriately be called 'the Acts of the Holy Spirit'.

There are some problems about the coming of the Spirit in Acts, since in some cases the fullness of the Spirit occurs at conversion and in other cases it appears to be a subsequent experience (compare Acts 8:17; 19:6). The former is the more usual and the instances of the latter should be interpreted in the light of these. It may be supposed that it was only at the point of the coming of the Spirit that the validity of faith was confirmed.

We may sum up the Acts evidence by noting that the activity of the Spirit in the life of the early church was a direct continuation of the Spirit's work in the life of Jesus and a direct fulfilment of his teaching about the Spirit.

The Spirit in the rest of the New Testament

It is in Paul's letters that considerable teaching is given about the Spirit and we will split this up into several sub-divisions for the sake of conciseness.

The Spirit in the church's mission

The impression created in Acts, that the Spirit was the dynamic agency in the work of evangelism, is reinforced in Paul's epistles. When Paul preached the gospel, he did so 'in demonstration of the Spirit' (1 Cor. 2:4). He did not rely on his own eloquence. Rather he spoke of his weakness. Another similar stress on the Spirit in proclamation is found in 1 Thessalonians 1:5 (compare also Eph. 3:5). There is no question of the development of the church in any other way than under the superintendence of the Spirit. This provides an important principle for church growth. Moreover, the Christians possess the 'sword of the Spirit', which is identified with the word of God (Eph. 6:17).

The Spirit initiates the Christian life

Paul takes it as an axiom that all believers are indwelt by the Spirit (1 Thess. 4:8; 1 Cor. 12:13). It is only through the Spirit that anyone can call Jesus 'Lord' (1 Cor. 12:3). No one belongs to Christ who does not have the Spirit (Rom. 8:9). Paul likens the Corinthians to God's temple in whom the Spirit dwells (1 Cor. 3:16).

The apostle uses the vivid metaphor of a seal to describe one aspect of the Spirit's presence (2 Cor. 1:22; 5:5; Eph. 1:13,14). He means that the gift of the Spirit now is an instalment which shows what is to follow. Once a person has the seal of the Spirit there is no dispute over ownership. That person no longer governs himself. He is set apart for God. In no clearer way could the apostle bring out the essential function of the Spirit in the believer. This continual emphasis underlines the work of the Spirit in re-birth.

The Spirit supports the Christian life

We shall make further comments on sanctification in a later section, but it is important to note that as the Spirit initiates the Christian life, so he continues to mould and lead the believer into greater conformity with Christ. In 2 Thessalonians 2:13 and 1 Corinthians 6:11, sanctification is definitely linked with the work of the Spirit. It may in fact be said that the main work of the Spirit is to develop the holy living of the believer.

This leads to a consideration of other activities of the Spirit, which may also be grouped under the general theme of sanctification.

Gives wisdom   One of the most important aspects is the illuminating of the mind. Paul sets out the special work of the Spirit in the giving of wisdom in 1 Corinthians 2:10–16. This is basic, in fact, to Paul's theological position, for he did not suppose that the unaided human mind was capable of grasping the revelation of God. In that revelation he recognised that there were depths which only the Spirit of God was able to probe. This truth is sufficient to humble the intellectually self-sufficient. The Christian life is seen as a constant realisation of new aspects of truth which the Spirit brings to light. The Christian acquires a new dimension – spiritual guidance for the mind. Paul does not hesitate to set spiritual wisdom over against human wisdom and shows the superiority of the former.

Gives assurance   The clearest exposition of the work of the Spirit in the life of the believer occurs in Romans 8, where there is a greater concentration of statements about the Spirit than anywhere else in the New Testament. We may sum up the Spirit's part in the new life in the following way. It is the Spirit who gives life (8:2,5). He dwells in the believer (8:9–11), which means that he comes as an honoured guest. Moreover, the Spirit acts as a guide (8:13,14) and deals with the problems of the old nature. The Spirit also assures believers that they are children of God (8:16). This is the basis of the Christian's experience of sonship. Such a thought also brings with it responsibilities, for those who are convinced they are sons must act as sons.

Intercedes   Perhaps the most remarkable statement about the Spirit in this passage is in Romans 8:26,27. This sets in perspective the Spirit's aid in the prayer life of the Christian. Paul recognises the difficulty of prayer, but assures his readers that the Spirit intercedes for them. The mode of that intercession is not easily grasped, for the apostle states that it is not in words. The depth of the intercession is measured by this fact. It is intended to be a great encouragement to those who find prayer difficult (and this must apply to most people at times). It is reassuring because the Spirit cannot intercede in a way which is contrary to God's will. His prayer on our behalf must always be answered.

Frees   Another important feature of the work of the Spirit is his activity in freeing those whose lives have been dominated by their own sin. This comes out not only in Romans 8:13, which shows that it is by the Spirit that sinful actions and impulses may be overcome, but also in Romans 8:21 which speaks of 'the glorious liberty' of the children of God. Freedom is said to be present where the Spirit is Lord (2 Cor. 3:17). Life lived under the control of the Spirit of God is therefore totally different from life lived under the control of the flesh. The Spirit breathes into life a marvellous sense of freedom, because the Christian life is not self-centred. In the decisions which the believer must make, the Spirit opposes self-centredness and superimposes an approach which will glorify Christ.

Strengthens   In various other ways Paul brings out the essential function of the Spirit in the Christian life. In speaking of the 'walk' of the Christian life – which he contrasts (Gal. 5:16) with pleasing the flesh – Paul thinks of the Spirit as setting the pattern for the Christian's footsteps. Walking in the Spirit means walking where the Spirit leads, and relying on the Spirit's strength. This latter point comes out more clearly in Ephesians 3:16, where Paul speaks of the inner man being strengthened by the Spirit. It is important to note that Paul never valued spiritual power for its own sake, but only for the fulfilment of God's purpose, both in the individual believer and in the community. In view of the importance attached to the Spirit's activity, it is no wonder that Paul should urge the believers to avoid 'grieving' the Spirit (Eph. 4:30), or 'quenching' the Spirit (1 Thess. 5:19), as this would amount to opposing the source of their spiritual dynamism.

Produces spiritual qualities   Another idea which appeals to Paul is that of growth. He can speak of the 'fruit' of the Spirit (Gal. 5:22,23), and the list he gives shows that the Spirit produces in the believer qualities which are of a kind greatly superior to those of the natural man. These qualities cannot be produced by mere self-cultivation. They spring from a source of life and vitality which is provided by the indwelling Spirit. We may link with this Galatians passage such statements which connect love with the Spirit (Rom. 5:5; Col. 1:8) or other qualities with the Spirit (Rom. 14:17). It seems fairly clear that Paul is thinking of specific qualities produced by the Spirit which are something more than an intensification of natural qualities. Love, joy and peace in a spiritual sense are a much deeper reality than those which are possessed by the natural man.

91

Enough has been said to show that the Christian life would be impossible without the continual activity of the Spirit in the believer. This leads on to a consideration of special aspects of the Spirit in the teaching of the apostle.

The unity of the Spirit

The New Testament never views the Spirit-led life in isolation. Believers belong to a body of people who are united in the Spirit (Phil. 2:1–4). Moreover, Christians are under an obligation to maintain the unity possessed by those who belong to the Spirit (Eph. 4:3,4). Paul cannot conceive of a situation in which those led by the Spirit could live together in a state of tension. The Spirit is a Spirit of peace and must therefore engender an attitude of peace among those in whom he dwells.

The baptism of the Spirit and the fullness of the Spirit

Much debate has surrounded the question whether Paul thought of a 'baptism' of, or in, the Spirit as being separate from the indwelling of the Spirit which takes place at conversion. We note first that nowhere in Paul's letters is there any exhortation to be baptised in the Spirit. In fact there is only one passage in which baptism and the Spirit are specifically linked together (1 Cor. 12:13), but even in this case the baptism is not said to be the work of the Spirit. Since in this passage baptism is said to be 'into one body', it is inconceivable that an experience distinct from and subsequent to conversion is in mind. There is no suggestion that anyone could be converted and yet not be part of the body.

The idea of being 'filled' with the Spirit is, on the other hand, a Pauline concept (Eph. 5:18). In this case the apostle is clearly thinking of a continuous experience for he uses the present tense. He cannot be referring to a once-for-all event which does not need repeating. Since he contrasts this with being drunk with wine, he is suggesting that there are degrees to which a person may be committed to the direction of the Spirit. A Spirit-filled person is one who allows the Spirit control over all aspects of life.

The Spirit as the giver of gifts

This is another subject which has been much debated. There is no dispute over the fact that the Spirit gives gifts. Three passages in Paul's letters make this clear – 1 Corinthians 12:8–11; 12:28; Ephesians 4:11. Questions arise over when the gifts are given, what is their nature, and whether all believers should possess all the gifts. From an examination of the evidence we may make the following observations. (i) There is a wide variety in the gifts which the Spirit gives, ranging from offices like apostles and evangelists, to special activities like healings and speaking with tongues. Since Paul varies both the content and the order in his lists, it is evident that he does not attach superior importance to any of the gifts. (ii) In the giving of the gifts the Spirit is sovereign and distributes according to his own will. (iii) The purpose of the gifts is for the edification of the church. Something more will be said about the importance of these gifts for the life of the church in the study on the latter topic. (iv) There would seem to be no support for the view that Paul held that every believer should exercise all the gifts.

We have been concentrating on Paul's teaching, but some of his salient points occur also in the remaining New Testament books. Believers possess the Spirit (compare Heb. 6:4; 1 Peter 1:2; Jude 19). The Spirit gives gifts (Heb. 2:4). The Spirit speaks through scripture (Heb. 3:7; 9:8; 10:15; 2 Pet 1:21). He has a part in Christ's sufferings (Heb. 9:14; compare 1 Pet. 1:10–12; 4:12–18). He deals both with individuals (Rev. 1:10; 4:2; 17:3; 21:10) and with churches (Rev. 2 and 3). Only in the book of Revelation is the Spirit described symbolically as 'seven' (Rev. 1:4; 3:1; 4:5; 5:6); this seems to indicate his perfection.

10

REPENTANCE AND FORGIVENESS

We have already seen, when discussing man's relation to God, that sin constitutes a barrier. Since sin is universal, it means that no one on earth, with the exception of Christ, has maintained uninterrupted fellowship with God. In view of the fact that man was made for God, it was imperative for some way to be found by which the barrier could be removed. We have already seen that one of the most important effects of the death of Christ was that it brought about a reconciliation between God and man. Our immediate question is how this possibility is turned into actuality in the experience of Christians. We shall consider the need for repentance and the provision for forgiveness.

Repentance

The first indication that the teaching of repentance was to be important to the mission of Jesus is that John the Baptist links his announcement of the coming kingdom with a call to repentance. He invited people to be baptised but only as a recognition that they repented of their sins. Although Jesus was himself without sin, he submitted to John's baptism because he wished to identify himself with those he had come to save. Moreover, Jesus began his own ministry with the same call to repentance (Mark 1:15). By repentance was meant an acknowledgement of guilt and a genuine sorrow for it. Repentance is a necessary prelude to receiving the blessings of the gospel. It certainly calls for humility and involves a decision. Because of this Jesus had no time for the self-righteous. He had come to call sinners to repentance (Luke 5:32), not righteous people, which suggests that the latter did not recognise the need for repentance.

When Jesus sent out his disciples on a mission they preached that people should repent (Mark 6:12). There is therefore a direct continuity between the proclamations of John the Baptist, of Jesus and of the disciples. The mission of Christ is meaningless to those who do not recognise their sin and do not turn to God in repentance. We note further that, in the parables of the lost coin and the lost sheep (compare Luke 15:7,10), Jesus mentioned that there is much joy in heaven over even one sinner who repents. Some have thought that the parable of the prodigal son raises a problem here because the father forgives before waiting for the son to repent, although the story implies that there is remorse on the son's part in that he confesses that he had sinned against heaven and against his father (Luke 15:18). The parable must not be pressed in every detail. Its purpose is not to give a treatise on reconciliation, for otherwise some indication of the basis of the father's forgiveness would be necessary. This parable speaks primarily of the father's love. Other New Testament teaching shows that forgiveness requires a basis in the death of Christ (see previous section).

When we pass from the Gospels to Acts and listen to the early preachers we find that the call to repentance is still prominent. On the day of Pentecost Peter concludes his sermon with an exhortation to 'repent and be baptised' (Acts 2:38). Baptism was the sequel to repentance, not vice versa. Peter makes repentance the prerequisite for times of refreshing (Acts 3:19). When brought before the religious authorities, he declared that God had worked through Christ to bring repentance to Israel (Acts 5:31). The same apostle recognised that God had granted repentance to the Gentiles (Acts 11:18, compare 26:20). At Athens, Paul boldly announced God's command to all men to repent (Acts 17:30). From this it is clear that repentance was an essential feature in the proclamation of the gospel. Only those who were willing to face the moral challenge of the gospel and were prepared to humble themselves before it could find acceptance. There is one tragic case in Acts where Ananias and Sapphira sinned, and neither of them were offered the opportunity to repent. No wonder great fear came upon the church (Acts 5:11). Yet when Simon, the former magician, was challenged over his wickedness, he was exhorted to repent and pray that the Lord might forgive him (Acts 8:22).

In view of all this emphasis on repentance, it is surprising that Paul says little about it in his epistles. The most likely explanation is that he takes for granted that those to whom he writes have already repented. When discussing the needs of Jews as well as Gentiles in Romans 2, he mentions that God's kindness is meant to lead to repentance (2:4). He recognises the part played by repentance in leading to salvation (2 Cor. 7:10). There is no suggestion that any meaningful relationship with God can be achieved apart from repentance. Where that is absent, man remains in his sins and the ultimate result is spiritual death.

We cannot leave the theme of repentance without noting that certain circumstances make repentance impossible. The case of the apostate in Hebrews 6:4–6 is significant here. The kind of person in mind is one who does not hesitate to hold Jesus Christ in contempt and, therefore, virtually to crucify him again. Repentance does not come to those who are so clearly antagonistic to God's provision of grace. Nevertheless, God is a God of mercy and does not wish that any should perish (2 Pet. 3:9). Those who reach a point of no return have only themselves to blame. Within the Christian church repentance is a constant need. Five of the seven churches addressed in Revelation 2 and 3 are exhorted to repent. Repentance is not only an essential need for unconverted people, but also a constant challenge to the children of God who have strayed from the purposes of God for them.

Forgiveness

In the New Testament repentance and forgiveness are closely linked. Forgiveness makes no sense unless there is acknowledgement of sin and real sorrow because of it. There is no suggestion that repentance is to be sought as an end in itself. There must always be the possibility of restoration. We need not repeat what was demonstrated in our discussion of the work of Christ that the death of Christ is the basis of God's forgiveness.

In the preaching of John the Baptist (Mark 1:4) and in the preaching of the early Christians (Acts 2:38; 5:31; 8:22; 26:18) forgiveness and repentance are mentioned together. Indeed, the risen Christ had reminded the disciples of their responsibility to witness to these truths (Luke 24:47).

Forgiveness formed an important theme in the ministry of Jesus. He reckoned forgiveness of sins to be more important than healing of the body (Mark 2:10). In this case, Jesus claimed authority to forgive sins in direct challenge to the contemporary Jewish belief that such authority belonged to God alone. In the parable of the prodigal son the father's forgiveness is a prominent feature although it is not the main point of the story (Luke 15). But it is the main point of the story of the unforgiving servant (Matt. 18:23–35). Moreover, the prayer for forgiveness included in the Lord's Prayer (Matt. 6:12; Luke 11:4) shows the importance that Jesus attached to it. It is challenging to note that the pattern appealed to is our willingness to forgive others. The reason for this seems to be that if we extend forgiveness to those who offend us, it will show we understand what we are asking for from God.

God's forgiveness is extended to all classes of wrongdoers. The Gospels record the case of the sinful woman who found forgiveness from Jesus and, as a result, anointed his feet (Luke 7:36–50). Jesus' willingness to forgive is in strong contrast to the Pharisee's desire to condemn. Forgiveness is not to be confused with a condoning of the sin. The most striking exhibition of a forgiving spirit is seen in Jesus himself when he prayed to God to forgive his murderers (Luke 23:34). Such forgiveness is characteristic of the gospel, which offers forgiveness and reconciliation to those who are at enmity with God. This feature comes out in the words spoken at the Lord's Supper in Matthew's record, where the blood is said to be poured out 'for the remission of sins' (Matt. 26:28). This makes clear the basis on which forgiveness can be granted.

There is one passage which has caused some to question whether they have committed the unpardonable sin. It is the so-called 'blasphemy saying' in which blasphemy against the Son of Man is forgiveable, but that against the Spirit is not (Mark 3:22–30). This saying is akin to the apostasy passage in Hebrews 6, mentioned above under 'repentance'. Those who blaspheme against the Spirit are those who attribute to Jesus the spirit of Beelzebub, a complete reversal of good and evil. It is no wonder that such a complete rejection of what Jesus was doing merited the severity of the impossibility of forgiveness. Such blasphemers would not want forgiveness. They reveal their hardened state of mind.

Before his ascension the risen Christ breathed over his disciples as he bestowed the Spirit on them and gave them power to forgive or retain sins (John 20:22,23). This cannot mean that they would be able to forgive on their own authority, for otherwise the presence of the Spirit would not be necessary. As already noted, the book of Acts shows these same disciples in action proclaiming forgiveness for those who believe in Jesus.

It is perhaps surprising that Paul says so little about forgiveness. In Ephesians 1:7 and Colossians 1:14 he links forgiveness with redemption. He sees no hope of forgiveness except through the blood of Christ. This gives us a clue to other aspects of what Christ has done. Paul's doctrine of reconciliation assumes a basis of forgiveness. His doctrine of justification also supports the reality of forgiveness, for if a person's standing before God is secured by faith in Christ there is no longer the threat of condemnation (Rom. 8:1). Sin is forgiven and the believer is acquitted of guilt because of Christ. It may be said, therefore, that forgiveness is a basic element in Paul's theology.

The same close connection between forgiveness and the shedding of blood, referring to Christ's death, is found again in Hebrews 9:22. Here there is a link between the Old Testament sacrificial system, which provided forgiveness, and the superior basis of forgiveness in Christ. Mention is also made of the new covenant, which assures the worshipper that God would remember their sins no more (8:12; 10:17). There is to be no sense of overhanging fate, no nagging guilt complex, because God has provided an adequate basis for forgiveness. This demonstrates the superiority of the new covenant over the old. The members of the new covenant (believers in Christ) are people who know that their sins are forgiven (compare 1 John 1:9; 2:12).

We have seen that those who repent and believe are forgiven and thus restored to a right relationship with God. We should perhaps reflect a little more on what the New Testament says about faith. The word 'faith' is used in a variety of different ways, but Paul's use is its most characteristic. For Paul, faith in Christ meant commitment to Christ. It involved a personal relationship. Sometimes Paul uses the word of the sum total of Christian teaching (as in the Pastoral epistles), but his more usual idea is of a dynamic and positive commitment to Christ. In John's Gospel there is no mention of faith, but many references to believing. In fact the purpose of the book is to lead readers to believe that Jesus is both Christ and Son of God (John 20:31). Believing is more than assenting to the truth of a statement, although this sense is found (John 14:11). A more penetrating idea of faith is that which involves trust or commitment (as in John 14:1).

There is a slightly different view of faith in Hebrews, especially in Hebrews 11:1–3. In the list of heroes in that chapter, faith has the quality of faithfulness and steadfastness. This is why the writer can not only appeal to Old Testament examples of faith, but can show their continuity with the faith of Christians. Nevertheless, this kind of faith is different from that initial act of believing which is the key to conversion. In this epistle the emphasis falls on

Christian hope rather than on faith as an act of commitment. It is faithful persistence in the godly life which is mainly in mind.

In James 2:14–17 the main purpose is to demonstrate the futility of claiming to have faith, if it does not lead to good works. Although it may seem that James is supporting salvation through works, this would be a wrong deduction because he recognises the need for faith as much as Paul (as Jas. 2:24 shows).

11

GOD'S INITIATIVE AND MAN'S RESPONSE

Election and free will

Since we have seen that salvation is available to those who repent and believe, there is clearly an importance attached to human response. We need to consider, therefore, what part is played by God's plan and purpose in all this. There has been much discussion over the relationship between God's sovereignty and man's free will. It will not be our purpose to enter into this debate, but the main passages on both sides must be briefly mentioned and some kind of assessment made of the New Testament teaching.

In the parables of Jesus there are many indications that mankind can be divided into two classes – those who respond and those who do not. The productive seed is contrasted with the non-productive, the wheat with the tares (Matt. 13:3–9,18–23,24–30, 36–43). There is no suggestion that the tares could ever turn into wheat. But does the parable of the wedding garment (Matt. 22:1–14) suggest that some might be cast out of the kingdom *after* they had entered? If the wedding garment is God's provision for the guests, anyone refusing that provision, thinking he could come on the strength of his own goodness, would exclude *himself* from salvation. There is no suggestion that the exclusion was in any sense arbitrary.

It is in John's Gospel that predestination comes more specifically into focus. It is quite clear that God took the initiative in man's salvation when he sent his Son. The Word became flesh (John 1:14). Believers received authority to become sons of God by the will of God (John 1:12). The new birth (John 3) clearly cannot be initiated by man. Jesus claimed that all that the Father gives him would come to him and that he would not cast out anyone who came to him (John 6:37; compare also verses 44, 65). In the passage where Jesus speaks metaphorically of his 'sheep', he says that no one will be able to snatch them out of his hand (John 10:28), which suggests that those who believe may have security, not because of their own efforts, but because of the Shepherd's care. There is no suggestion that the sheep would be left to their own devices. The Shepherd's love and concern for them is too great for that. In John 15:16 Jesus states that the disciples did not choose him, but that he chose them. This at once leads us to the problem of the divine choice. We are given no indication why God chooses, but there is no denying that he does. The theoretical question whether those chosen can reject God's choice is not discussed. There is one passage which may suggest the possibility of falling away – the allegory of the vine where the fruitless branches are lopped off (John 15:6). One of the most perplexing instances of choice is the case of Judas (John 6:70). Why did Jesus choose a man he knew would give in to the devil? There is no easy answer. Indeed, the key is locked up in the mind of Jesus. Judas was chosen to be a member of the itinerant group of disciples, but this clearly did not carry with it a guarantee of salvation.

The fullest statements in the New Testament, bearing on predestination, are found in Paul's epistles. The classic passage is Romans 8:28–30, in which Paul states that God predestined 'those whom he foreknew'. In spite of the difficulties raised by this passage there can be no doubt that the apostle intends his readers to understand that the outcome of God's provision of salvation is not left to man. He revels in the conviction that God takes the initiative. He has known it in his own life. He does not discuss the position of those who reject God's offer of salvation. He never speaks of the predestination of unbelievers. Other passages in Paul where a similar theme occurs are Romans 8:33 and Colossians 3:12, where he speaks of the 'elect', and Ephesians 1:4,5, where he speaks of God's choice and purpose. Indeed, the whole section of Ephesians 1:3–14, is full of references to God's plan.

How does all this fit into man's free will? Paul again does not discuss the matter. But it would not seem likely to him that man could interfere with God's plan. This confronts us with a mystery for there is no evidence either that Paul thought of man as a mere puppet. In some way he held man's responsibility and God's sovereignty in balance. He believed firmly that believers may be sure of their salvation (compare Eph. 1:13,14). The theme of Christian assurance would make little sense if man's actions can thwart God's plan.

In Hebrews there are two passages which presuppose the possibility of falling away (Heb. 6:1–12 and 10:26–39). One speaks of re-crucifying the Son of God and the other of spurning the Son of God. For such people no repentance is possible. But how could anyone once enlightened by the Holy Spirit reach such a state of apostasy? It should be noted that there is no suggestion in the epistle that anyone had yet reached such a state. But if it is a possibility, is it intelligible to speak of the sovereignty of God in individual lives? In the same epistle which mentions this apostasy possibility, however, there are many passages which speak of hope and the full assurance of faith (compare Heb. 3:6; 10:22). Again, there is no hint of tension. Many other warning passages occur in addition to those mentioned above (for example, Heb. 2:1–4; 3:7–19; 12:12–17) which also stress the responsibility of man in responding to God's call. In view of the existence of passages side by side in this epistle which stress both the possibility of falling away and of full assurance, it is difficult to resolve the matter in any logical way.

Peter writes of God choosing his people (1 Pet. 1:2), and he calls God's people a 'chosen race' (2:9,10). In the latter case the 'chosen' are contrasted with those who 'stumble' over Christ. The calling of God is also strongly present in 2 Peter (1:10) and in Jude (verse 1), although warnings are given about the dangers of false teachers. In the book of Revelation there is a division between those sealed with the mark of the Lamb and those sealed with the mark of the beast (compare Rev. 7:1–8; 13:16–18), and there is no suggestion that those once sealed by God would fall away.

The New Testament therefore presents two parallel lines of approach. It stresses that God is working his purposes out; thus his people may have confidence in his sovereign ability to carry out his designs. But it also presents challenges to people to respond to the call of God and makes clear the consequences of not doing so. If we follow the New Testament pattern we shall have to leave unresolved any tension which arises. We know that we are accountable to God, but we also know that God is our security.

The Christian life

When considering the nature of the Christian life into which believers are initiated at conversion, we must first examine the dominant motives. Since the Christian is a new creature, he needs new sources of power to develop within him the principles of the new nature which he has received. These new resources are described in the New Testament in various ways.

Love   There is no doubt that the most powerful incentive is love. The believer's pattern for love towards others is no less than the love of Christ for him (John 15:12). The motive power of love is particularly stressed in John's Gospel, especially in chapters 14–17. It is even stronger in 1 John (compare 3:11–18; 4:7–12; 5:1–2). In the epistles of Paul we find the same emphasis. God works everything for good for those who love him (Rom. 8:28). But men are also expected to love their neighbours (Rom. 13:8). Believers are to love continually as Christ loved them (Eph. 5:2). The overwhelming power of love is most eloquently expressed in Paul's great hymn of love in 1 Corinthians 13. The idea that life can be dominated by love was certainly a new concept in New Testament times, and it remains a principle which cannot be excelled by the non-Christian world. Nevertheless, if the Christian church was intended to be a group of people who demonstrate their love for each other in a way which impresses the world, it must be admitted that the ideal has all too often been obscured.

'In Christ' and 'in the Spirit'   Another powerful principle is the close connection between the believer and Christ, which is especially expressed by Paul in the formula 'in Christ' or 'in the Spirit'. These expressions are important because they reveal much of the new quality of life granted to the Christian. His life is no longer centred on self, but in Christ. Paul speaks of the believer being 'baptised into Christ' (Rom. 6:3) and links it with being 'baptised into his death'. Some kind of death experience is necessary before newness of life can be known. The new life into which the believer is baptised has, moreover, a corporate aspect – it is an experience shared with others (1 Cor. 12:13). All are baptised into one body. To be 'in Christ' is to be one with all others who are 'in Christ'.

It is because the believer is 'in Christ' that he is a new creature (2 Cor. 5:17). What does this mean? Does it simply stand for 'Christian'? It certainly means that, but it also means considerably more. The new creation is wholly Christ-dominated; the old life has been put off. There is also an element of mysticism in the expression 'in Christ', as if Christ is the environment in which the believer now lives. This does not mean, of course, that the believer's natural environment is of no consequence. Those in Christ have all the more reason for living an increasingly moral life. If they are in Christ their spiritual strength comes from Christ.

There are a number of different ways in which 'in Christ' is applied by Paul. He speaks of us being *justified in Christ* (Gal. 2:17) or *sanctified in Christ* (1 Cor. 1:2); in these cases the expression points to Christ as the one who is involved in the process. He is the agent through whom God justifies and sanctifies. Paul often uses the word to suggest *incorporation* into Christ (for example Romans 8:2). He sees *redemption* as rooted in Christ (Rom. 3:24). He can also speak of the Christian's *wisdom* as in Christ (1 Cor. 4:10). Everything about the Christian life is determined by its 'in Christ' quality, which contrasts so vividly with the 'in Adam' quality of the natural man. Paul clearly brings this out in 1 Corinthians 15:20–22.

He sometimes uses the expression 'in the Spirit' in much the same way as 'in Christ' (compare Rom. 8:9). Since he uses the two expressions in the same context, it is clear that he makes a close connection between the two. Some have even claimed that Paul drew no distinction between Christ and the Spirit (compare 2 Cor. 3:17), but this view leads to confusion. He certainly saw that the believer's resources were as essentially in the Spirit as in Christ. We shall note below the indispensable part played by the Spirit in the sanctification of the believer.

Christ lives in the Christian   Closely akin to the teaching just mentioned is that which speaks of 'the indwelling Christ' or 'the indwelling Spirit'. For the apostle, Christian experience amounts to Christ living within (Gal. 2:20) or the Spirit living within (Rom. 8:9). It is not surprising that this idea makes great demands on the believer. With Christ as a guest the life of the believer must be affected to the extent that his moral behaviour must be in harmony with the indwelling Christ. Christians are no longer controlled by the sinful nature, but by the Spirit who lives in them (Rom. 8:9). When Paul writes of the believer as being a temple of the Holy Spirit (1 Cor. 6:19), he reminds the Corinthians that they are not their own, but are bought with a price. It is presumably with this idea in mind that Paul can use a different metaphor and can speak of the believer 'putting off' the old man and 'putting on' Christ (Rom. 13:14; Gal. 3:27).

From these indications in the Pauline epistles, it is clear that

Paul sees the Christian life in terms which differ radically from the life of the natural man. The new creature in Christ is motivated by an entirely new standard of values.

Paul is not alone in stressing this kind of indwelling teaching. Jesus had already spoken to his disciples about 'abiding' in him (John 15:1-11), using the allegory of the vine to illustrate his point. The branches have no life in themselves and can certainly not produce fruit. It is only in so far as they remain in the vine (that is, in Christ) that they can hope to fulfil their true function. This shows the total dependence of Christians on Christ as the source not only of their life but of their continued development. The most remarkable promise that Jesus makes in this passage is that those who abide in him may ask what they will and it shall be done (John 15:7), which shows that abiding in Christ means a conformity to the mind of Christ so that any requests are not out of harmony with him.

This idea of abiding in Christ exercised a powerful influence over John, as the use of the same concept in 1 John shows. The pattern of Christ's life becomes a pattern for those abiding in him (1 John 2:6). They must also observe his commandments (1 John 3:24). They are further exhorted not to sin (1 John 3:6). The secret is to identify with Christ to such a degree that he becomes the pattern for the new life.

There is little emphasis on this particular aspect of the believer's new life in the rest of the New Testament. We may say, therefore, that it is almost entirely confined to Paul's and John's writings.

Sanctification

The term 'sanctification' is used to describe the process by which the believer becomes increasingly conformed to the image of Christ. The word comes from a root meaning 'to set apart for a holy purpose' and this sums up the goal for the New Testament believer. Although it is sometimes used of an act completed (in the sense of justification, as in 1 Cor. 6:11), it is more generally presented as something to be attained. Jesus taught that men should be perfect as their heavenly Father is perfect (Matt. 5:48). This seems such an impossible demand that one wonders in what sense Jesus intended it. No one could attain to the perfection of the Father, if the purity of his character is in mind. The context refers to love and it is possible that the Father's perfection of love is intended, but even then the pattern is manifestly out of reach. It should be noted that the word 'perfect' here properly means 'complete' or 'mature', features which are seen pre-eminently in the Father.

In other parts of the sermon on the mount Jesus sets out certain aims for the disciples, especially in the Beatitudes. Such qualities as humility and compassion, which are not highly rated by the natural man, become the norm. Attitudes towards others are due for radical change, for even enemies must be loved (Matt. 5:44). It is clear from the sermon on the mount that Jesus set his sights high for his disciples. The Christian life was to involve a progressive transformation.

In the teaching of Jesus in John's Gospel there are various indications of ways to promote the development of the spiritual life. Observance of the commandments of Jesus, especially the command to love one another, is seen to be important (John 14:15; 15:12,17). Jesus sees himself and the Father as patterns for Christian behaviour (compare John 13:15; 15:9,12). He even refers to the act of sanctifying himself (John 17:19), which seems to refer to his dedication to his mission. But the same word which he uses for himself is that which he applies to the disciples (John 17:17).

Two other important factors in the process of sanctification are the need for purification (the moral factor) and the work of the Holy Spirit (the dynamic factor). In the allegory of the vine the old branches need purging out in order to increase the yield (John 15:2), and this is used to illustrate a principle of spiritual growth: the process of discarding anything which inhibits the full development of a holy life. Moreover, this aspect of sanctification is not something which happens once only: it is a continuous process, as the verb in the present tense (John 15:2) shows.

In John's Gospel, more than anywhere else in the teaching of Jesus, stress is put on the work of the Holy Spirit in the life of the believer. The Spirit brings new life (John 3:3,5). This must involve a totally new way of life. But the Spirit is promised as an indwelling guest (John 14:17) and as a teacher (John 14:26). There is no suggestion that the believers would be left to their own devices. Indeed, it is assumed that they must rely wholly on the Spirit.

When we turn from the teaching of Jesus to that of the apostles, we discover a fuller exposition of the processes which have their roots in that teaching. As in our discussion of the new life, it is Paul's epistles which preserve most of this kind of teaching. Paul distinguishes the process of sanctification from the act of justification. The latter is an accomplished reality, whereas the former needs working out (compare Phil. 2:12,13). Paul makes very clear, however, that God must work as well as man in the process.

We have already noted that he recognises the powerful motive of love in controlling Christian behaviour and fostering the sanctifying process. In 1 Corinthians 13 he sets out clearly the effects of Christian love. It produces such fruits as patience, kindness, tolerance and joy, which are also aspects of the fruit of the Spirit (compare Gal. 5:22,23). It is remarkable that the apostle attaches more importance to love than to any of the gifts of the Spirit mentioned in 1 Corinthians 12–14. To him, love is a more powerful motive than the more spectacular ecstatic gifts.

Another important factor in the right development of the Christian life is the contribution of the mind. In an age which was long before the rise of the scientific study of human behaviour, Paul recognised the dominant part played by the mind in directing the body. He speaks of the need for the 'renewal' of the mind (Rom. 12:2), for only a renewed mind can understand the will of God. He exhorts his readers to set their minds on doing the things the Spirit requires (Rom. 8:5). When writing to the Philippians he wants them to have 'the same mind' – all of them sharing the attitudes of Christ – and goes on to illustrate what he means by referring to 'the mind of Christ' (Phil. 2:1–11). He closes his letter to these same people with an appeal to them to think about the noblest things (Phil. 4:8,9). In Colossians 3:2 he puts the matter in another way – set your mind on higher things. The importance of mental attitudes in sanctification is particularly evident in Paul's writings. While he does not neglect the emotional aspect, he is convinced that the springs of action are in the mind rather than the affections. He would have agreed with the adage – 'as a man thinks, so he is'. The purer the thought, the purer the life will be.

The apostle was at pains to stress the human as well as the divine side of sanctification. The passage from Philippians 2:12,13, already cited, brings this out clearly – 'work out your own salvation with fear and trembling'. But other passages bring out the same point (compare Rom. 6:19; 1 Thess. 4:3). There must clearly be an effort on man's part, although the divine working is still real. The Holy Spirit is especially promised as an aid in the process of sanctification (compare Rom. 15:16; 1 Thess. 4:7,8; 2 Thess. 2:13). The Spirit's activity is geared to the production of greater holiness in the believer. Although the standard is high, there is every incentive and an effective means for achieving it.

One matter of some importance which arises from Paul's teaching is the question of whether he supports the idea of sinless perfection, the doctrine that it is possible in this life to achieve perfection. The main passage which comes under discussion is

Romans 6:1–11. Paul cannot see how anyone who has died to sin can still live in sin. He maintains that anyone who has died to sin is no longer enslaved to sin (compare 6:6,7,14,22). Do these statements imply the possibility of complete sinlessness? Paul does not say that they do. He is content to show that sin has lost its mastery, but he is not so blind as to suppose that the Christian will not have to wage continuous war against the incursions of sin into his own life.

It would seem reasonable to suppose that Paul sees the perfecting of believers as the ultimate goal of the Christian life, but that he is only too aware of his own spiritual shortcomings to think that present perfection is a probability. He emphatically denies in Philippians 3:12 that he is already perfect, but is nevertheless pressing on towards that goal (Phil. 3:14). Since he is convinced that every believer will be presented to God 'blameless and holy' (1 Thess. 3:13, NIV) he clearly sees a close connection between justification and sanctification. In the presence of God they will coincide. Paul's favourite word for Christians is 'saints' or 'holy ones', which describes them in an ideal sense. Because the Holy Spirit dwells within them they are a holy temple (1 Cor. 6:19; Eph. 2:21).

There are some passages in 1 John which again raise the issue of sinless perfection. John says that no one who abides in him (that is, Christ), sins (1 John 3:6), which certainly looks like support for sinless perfection as a norm. Two other statements (1 John 3:9 and 5:18) appear to agree with this. But all three of these statements express the verb in the present tense, which implies that believers do not go on sinning as a *habitual* process. If this is the right interpretation it would not mean that Christians never commit acts of sin. In any case, according to 1 John 1:9; 2:1,2, provision is made for the forgiveness of those who sin. Moreover, since in this epistle John says quite specifically that those who say they have no sin deceive themselves (1 John 1:8), it is clear that sinless perfection is ruled out. Although there seems to be a paradox, the apparent contradiction is resolved if it is supposed that a Christian cannot accept habitual sinning but, if he commits acts of sin, he knows that a way of forgiveness is provided. Certainly perfection is to be the Christian's goal.

This goal of perfection is seen in Hebrews where the concept occurs several times. Because Jesus is himself said to be perfect it is not surprising that the Christian's aim is also to be perfect (compare 5:9). Even the heroes of faith of a past age are shown as aiming at perfection, but falling short of it (Heb. 11:40). However, there is no suggestion that perfection can be attained through human effort. Indeed, the only one who is spoken of as perfect is Jesus Christ and even he is not said to make himself perfect: it is the work of God (Heb. 2:10). One of the major points made in the epistle to the Hebrews is that the law could make nothing perfect (Heb. 7:19). It took the blood of Jesus to sanctify his people (Heb. 13:12). The readers are left in no doubt that God's purpose for them is to bring them to perfection. The concluding benediction shows this (Heb. 13:20). Those who know that perfection has not yet been attained nevertheless know that God has undertaken to bring the process of sanctification to completion. When the writer speaks of the 'heavenly Jerusalem', he sees among the worshippers the spirits of just men already made perfect (Heb. 12:23). This shows the goal as having been achieved.

The New Testament contains a number of lists which give some indication of the virtues expected to be developed in the process of sanctification. Paul has a number of these (for example, Gal. 5:22,23; Eph. 4:25–32; Col. 3:12–17). But other writers also include them (compare Jas. 3:17; 1 Pet. 3:8,9; 2 Pet. 1:5–11). These qualities are of a high moral order and show the nature of the demands made on every Christian. Indeed, Peter cites from the Old Testament the high pattern 'You shall be holy, for I am holy' (1 Pet. 1:16).

12

THE LAW AND THE COVENANT

The New Testament presents the Christian life under the concept of a new covenant. Against the Old Testament background of God's covenantal dealings with Israel, the New Testament sees that God has entered into a new agreement with his people, not confined to Israel but embracing people of all nations. We shall note the major features of this teaching for it will enable us to assess the place of the law in the Christian life.

A new covenant
The idea of a new covenant was clearly predicted in Jeremiah 31:31–34, the main significance of which was that God's law would be written on men's hearts rather than on tablets of stone. It was to be an internal law which would govern people's actions. This passage is quoted at length in Hebrews 8 in demonstrating the superiority of the new covenant over the old. Clearly what had become part of a person's way of thinking was superior to what was merely external.

'In his blood'   This new covenant was not introduced, however, without cost. Jesus spoke of it as a covenant 'in his blood' to be commemorated in the words of institution which he introduced at the Supper (Matt. 26:28). The connection between the covenant and the death of Christ is of great importance in establishing the

Christian's approach to it. Those who attach any less value to the blood of Christ will fail to appreciate the centrality of the new covenant.

'In the Spirit'   Paul develops this theme in 2 Corinthians 3, where he declares that the Christian ministry is a ministry of a new covenant which is 'in the Spirit'. Its splendour far outshines the old covenant; so much so that the old loses what splendour it had by comparison.

A 'better' covenant   The writer to the Hebrews sees Jesus as the surety of this 'better' covenant (7:22). He had just established that the old could make nothing perfect and was accordingly weak (compare 7:18). He later goes on to speak of Jesus as mediator of a better covenant (8:6; 9:15; 12:24). This new covenant is the basis of a more effective relationship between God and man. The Christian knows that the intercession of his High Priest is infinitely more effective, because it is continuous and because Christ has no need to intercede for himself (Heb. 4:15; 7:25). As Jesus himself had done, this writer connects the sealing of the covenant with blood (9:15–28; 13:20), again adding a note of great solemnity to it. Indeed, he pronounces the severest condemnation on any who would regard the blood of the covenant lightly (Heb. 10:29).

The Law

In view of this emphasis on the new covenant introduced by Jesus, a question arises over the extent to which the law, which was the expression of the old covenant, has any continuing relevance for the Christian. This is an important matter for it involves the whole question of the Christian approach to the Old Testament. We need to know what the New Testament says about the law, especially about what parts of the law are still valid. Has the gospel entirely done away with law? Has law any function in an age of grace? To answer these questions we shall concentrate on what Jesus said about it and what lines of interpretation Paul gives.

It is important to examine Jesus' approach to the law, since it is reasonable to suppose that his attitude formed the pattern for the disciples' attitude. In some statements Jesus pointed to the weakness of the law and in others to its value. If we take the latter aspect first we shall need to take special note of one passage in the sermon on the mount (Matt. 5:17,18). In this, Jesus' high view of the law is inescapable. He declared that no part of the law would pass away until all that it prophesied and foreshadowed had been accomplished. Does this mean, therefore, that the Christian is still under the law? There is no denying that Jesus was claiming a continuing validity for the law. The fact that he claimed to fulfil it shows the importance he attached to it. This may, in fact, give some indication of the part to be played by the law in the Christian life. If the law provided a pattern or yardstick by which Christ's own life could be pronounced sinless, it has the same function for the Christian.

Since Jesus was a Jew and the disciples were Jews, a high regard for the law is understandable. But we shall need to balance this with the approach to the law in Paul's epistles, which were largely written against a Gentile background. Jesus expected observance of the commandments, although he was careful to show in what sense he interpreted the law. Compare, for instance, the 'eye for an eye' approach of the law and the advice of Jesus to his followers to turn the other cheek (Matt. 5:38–42). In this case, as in many others, he was bringing out the true meaning of the law. It should be noticed, however, that alongside his high regard for the law, he acknowledged its weakness. He did not hesitate to ignore the ritual law, as when he touched a leper, or did what was considered by his critics to be work on the sabbath which, according to the current Pharisaic interpretation of the law, was not allowed. Jesus, with all his regard for the law, was never legalistic in his approach, but was strongly critical of the scribes and Pharisees for being so (Matt. 23).

Because the Jews reckoned that anyone who broke a part of the law was guilty of breaking the whole, it is understandable why they took such a strong line over Jesus' attitude to the sabbath. In John 5:1–18 the case of sabbath breaking revolved around the healing of a paralysed man, although the main bone of contention was over what Jesus himself was claiming to be and to do. A similar case of sabbath healing occurs in John 9 and again the narrative leads on to a statement about the nature of Jesus (vs. 35–41). When he declared that 'the sabbath was made for man, not man for the sabbath' (Mark 2:27), Jesus established a principle which throws light on the Christian approach to the law and its purpose.

When the apostles came to reflect on the important question of what Christians should do in relation to the law, there was a firm conviction that Jesus himself had introduced a new approach. In his prologue John says that, whereas law came through Moses, grace and truth came through Christ (John 1:17). John is not denying that the law has validity, but that God's provision in Christ goes beyond the law. This is in keeping with Paul's view that the law could not provide man with salvation.

In the book of Acts we see that two questions arose regarding the law. First, Stephen was accused of opposing the law (Acts 6:11,13). It is clear that his Jewish opponents put a wrong construction on the fact that Christians claimed to be liberated from the law. For those for whom the law was sacrosanct the idea that salvation could come apart from the law was inconceivable. It appeared to them to be blasphemy. But, second, even Christian Jews had problems over the law, as Acts 15 shows. The issue came to a head because Gentiles had become Christians and the Jewish believers thought they should be circumcised. This was a natural conclusion since the law required it of Jewish proselytes, but it was nevertheless wrong, as the apostles came to realise. It was an important move forward when it was decided that the new converts should not be in bondage to the laws of Judaism, but only to the rule of Christ.

Paul has a great deal to say about the law and it will be possible here to give only a brief summary of his views. He certainly recognised the value of the law and could describe it as holy (Rom. 7:12). For him it was holy because it had a holy source (that is, God). Nevertheless, becoming a Christian changed his approach to the law. He no longer regarded it as a binding written code ('the written code kills': 2 Cor. 3:6), because he was now under submission to the law of Christ. This implies freedom from the entanglements of the law (Gal. 5:1). The Christian is not intended to have a legalistic approach. He is expected to keep God's commandments, but the motivation for doing so is love (compare Rom. 13:9). If God's commands, expressed in the Decalogue, are seen to be the provision of God's grace, obedience to them ceases to be a burden.

It is not surprising, however, that some of the early Christians had problems about the law. Such problems, for instance, arose in the Galatian churches and in Colossae because of an over-legalistic approach to the law. But the apostle was insistent on the liberty which Christians should enjoy.

If we ask what Paul's view was of the function of the law, the answer will be varied. He sees it as bringing an understanding of sin (Rom. 3:20; 7:7). But at the same time it stimulates sin (Rom. 5:20; 7:13). The idea seems to be that any prohibition leads to resistance in the corrupt mind. But this would not be true of the Christian. For it is only a person already biased towards sin who would want to break the law and so increase the law's condemnation of him. Yet for the Christian, law is a spiritual agency. It must not be forgotten that Paul sees some aspects of the law as burdensome, because it commits a man to observe it in its entirety (Gal. 3:10). When he says that the law was our 'tutor' until Christ came (Gal. 3:24), he is showing that it changed its function after the coming of Christ. He can even say that Christ is the end of the law (Rom. 10:4).

The epistle to the Hebrews shows a rather different interest in the law. It is concerned to show the fulfilment of the ceremonial aspects of the law and to demonstrate the superior efficacy of Christ's work to that of the law. The sacrificial system no longer applies to Christians, because Christ has become the perfect sacrifice. They no longer need priests to intercede, because Christ is the perfect High Priest. Hebrews even states that the law has become obsolete (Heb. 8), presumably in the sense that it does not play the same integral part in the new covenant as it did in the old.

To sum up, we may say that the law still has validity as part of the total revelation of God, although the Christian is delivered from a legalistic bondage to it.

13

THE CHURCH

The New Testament never presents the Christian life as a purely individual experience. The church is not something imposed on believers. It is integral to their growth and usefulness. We shall consider this aspect of corporate Christian living under two sections: first, what Jesus taught about it, and then what the apostolic writings have to say about it.

The church in the teaching of Jesus
There is so little specifically about the church in the Gospels that some have maintained that Jesus had little interest in it. But there is enough evidence to dispense with that view. The fact that the early Christians, almost immediately after the resurrection of Jesus, grasped the importance of the community idea suggests that it must have had some basis in Jesus' own teaching. It is, moreover, highly unlikely that he in no way prepared his disciples for the future. It must therefore be recognised that the few direct references should be regarded as definite pointers.

Unity and community   We have already noted how much Jesus said about the kingdom of God and this is clearly a community idea. We have also noted the question about the relation between the kingdom and the church. They cannot be identified, but neither can they be dissociated. If we regard the kingdom as wider

117

than the church we can include within it all the people of God in all ages. It is reasonable to suppose that many of the principles brought out in the teaching on the kingdom are in that case applicable to the church. Certainly the manifestation of the kingdom in this age is seen in the activity of the church.

There are some other considerations of a preliminary kind which support the idea that Jesus presupposed a community which would carry on the work which he had begun. He chose a specific group of followers, whom he named 'apostles' (Matt. 10:2; Luke 6:13). In addition there were many others who simply went by the name of 'disciples'. The followers of Jesus formed a separate group distinct from other people. In John's Gospel the idea of the unity of God's people is strongly brought out. His people would be gathered into one community (John 11:52). In Jesus' prayer for his disciples in John 17 the idea of unity is specially affirmed (compare John 17:22). These emphases on unity cannot support individualism and must point to a coming community, which would find a common basis in Christ himself. The kind of oneness which Jesus had in mind was no less than the oneness which existed between himself and his Father. John includes two allegories which both show the importance of the community idea. That of the shepherd and the flock particularly brings out the importance of the one flock, although admitting the existence of different folds (John 10:16). There is certainly a universal character about the coming community. The other allegory, that of the vine, brings out the community aspect even more clearly, in that all the fruitful branches are united in the one stem, that is, Christ (John 15). In John's Gospel the basis of community is, in fact, a common faith in Christ, a faith which is otherwise described in terms of abiding in Christ.

Composition and universality   When we consider the specific references to the church in the teaching of Jesus, we discover that the word 'church' occurs only twice, both times in Matthew's Gospel. It may seem surprising that the other Gospels omit all reference to it, but it is evidently of special interest to Matthew. The omissions from the others cannot be regarded as evidence that the theme of the church was unimportant. The widespread interest in it in the apostolic writings would not support such a view. The relevant passages in Matthew are 16:18 and 18:17 and these raise several significant issues.

The first question is over the interpretation of the word 'church' in these two contexts. The root meaning of the word is 'called out'. It was used in the Greek Old Testament of the congregation of Israel. But the teaching of Jesus was never narrowly Jewish. The word on his lips is more expansive and includes all those who were to become his followers, represented immediately by his disciples. Since Jesus declared that he was going to build his church 'on the rock' it is important, secondly, to arrive at a right understanding of the 'rock'. Peter's name means 'rock' and the question arises whether Jesus intended to say that his church was to be founded on Peter. This cannot be established from the play on words, although the important part assigned to Peter cannot be denied. The best interpretation is to suppose that the rock was *Peter as confessor that Jesus was the Christ*, the Son of the living God, in that the church would consist only of those who similarly confessed Christ. Another aspect of the same saying is the declaration that Peter would be given 'the keys' of the kingdom. It is significant that Peter was the first person to open the door both to Jewish believers (Acts 2) and to Gentile believers (Acts 10). But the 'keys' are also connected with the promise to Peter that he would bind and loose. This probably relates to the forgiveness of sins, since this idea occurs also in John 20:23. But Jesus did not intend to invest this authority solely in Peter, as Matt. 18:18 shows. The whole passage demonstrates that Jesus himself would superintend his community ('I will build'). The words give no clear indication of any church organisation. The second passage (Matt. 18:17) refers to disciplinary action within the church, but again gives no indication of the organisation. Its significance is that some corporate body of people is clearly in mind.

There is one other aspect of Jesus' teaching in Matthew which has some bearing on the church, that is the commission to the disciples in Matthew 28:18–20. This passage promises the presence of Jesus with his people. It also exhorts the early Christians to make disciples 'of all nations', which shows that Jesus planned that his church should be universal. Moreover, the disciples were to be taught Jesus' commands, which points to the importance of a well-taught community. Luke includes a farewell commission, but it is not expressed in such specific terms as in Matthew (compare Luke 24:45–49).

'Lord's Supper' and baptism   It must be noted that all the Synoptic Gospels record the way in which Jesus introduced the Last Supper. He intended it to be an interpretation of his death. Although nothing is said in the Gospels about the regular repetition of the Supper as a part of the worship procedures in the church, it can

hardly be maintained that it was intended to have significance only for the disciples on one specific occasion. In any case the wording in Paul's account in 1 Corinthians 11:23–26 twice contains the expression, 'Do this in remembrance of me'. Moreover, the practice of the early church shows a regular observance of the act. John's Gospel omits altogether the institution of the Supper, although he includes some teaching of Jesus about the bread which helps to explain the meaning (John 6:51–56). It is clear from this passage that the act of participation in the Supper has significance only for believers, that is, those who are abiding in Christ (v.56).

The other act which Jesus inaugurated was baptism, although it was the disciples who performed the act (John 4:2). There were, of course, precedents. John the Baptist baptised, and in some respects Jesus carried on along the same lines. Indeed, he submitted himself to John's baptism, evidently to show his identification with his contemporaries, in spite of the fact that he had no need for repentance. Since a command to baptise is included in the commission mentioned above, there is no doubt that Matthew recognised that Jesus expected the act of baptism to continue into the church age. In John 3:5 there may be an allusion to baptism in the reference to being 'born of water' but not all interpreters would agree about this. Of more importance is the fact that if baptism is in mind the spiritual dimension is most emphasised.

Work and witness   Although there is no mention of the church in John's Gospel there are quite a number of indirect indications which bear on the New Testament doctrine of the church. Certainly the powerful operation of the Holy Spirit, whose activity is specially stressed in John (chs. 14–16), is an essential feature of the work and witness of the Christian community. This aspect of the church is particularly developed in the epistles. Other features are the pointers towards Christian ministry which are seen in the preparation of the twelve (compare John 1:42; 6:68,69; this feature is also seen in the Synoptics), the door and the shepherd allegories (John 10), and the special commission to Peter which also uses the sheep imagery (John 21). From these passages we may note that the servants of Christ do not appoint themselves; they are expected to have as loving a concern for others as the shepherd has for his sheep; they are to protect and to feed the sheep. These various activities all contribute to the total New Testament picture of the pastoral office. Jesus recognised the ease with which counterfeit shepherds would arise and warns against such. He also knew that the under–shepherds he had appointed were (like Peter) fallible people. He was clearly not relying on their expertise. He was concerned chiefly about their relation to him and their concern for others. He expected them to show humility, as is clear from the example he set them when he washed their feet (John 13). Indeed, the conclusion that the Christian ministry is essentially one of service is inescapable.

The church in action in the book of Acts

It is to the book of Acts that we must turn for an account of the establishment of the church.

Community of the Spirit   The descent of the Holy Spirit on the community of the disciples in the upper room marked God's inauguration of the church. This theme of the fullness and activity of the Holy Spirit runs throughout the book. The most casual reader could not fail to be impressed with the fact that the church was clearly the community of the Spirit. It should also be noted that the most deep-rooted conviction of the early Christians was that God had turned the death of Jesus to good account through the resurrection. This conviction formed the basis of the preaching of the gospel at the very beginning. It was on the strength of this victory that the message of repentance was proclaimed. The early church was God–initiated and God–motivated.

At its commencement the community was almost entirely Jewish, but this pattern rapidly changed as the gospel spread to Gentile areas. The switch was not without considerable difficulties, since the Jewish Christians still felt some affinities with their Jewish heritage and found it hard to imagine that Gentiles could be full Christians without submitting to circumcision. The matter was resolved, however, when the apostles, elders and church members decided, under the direction of the Holy Spirit, that Gentiles need not be circumcised. It was a decision which had far-reaching consequences, for it liberated the Christian community from being tied to the ritual procedures of the past.

Practices   The early Christians rapidly developed distinctive behaviour patterns. They showed such love for each other that they shared meals together, a sharing which soon extended to the idea of common possessions (Acts 2:44–47; 4:32–35). This happened spontaneously and was clearly not obligatory. The case of Ananias and Sapphira sufficiently demonstrates this. The development of the Christian community in this communal way was a natural expression of Christian unity.

121

Other patterns which at once showed themselves were the practices of baptism and the breaking of bread together, two acts which were to play an important part in the procedures of the church. Since we have no record of any corporate decision to observe these ordinances, we must assume that baptism was followed because of the direct command of the risen Lord, and that the observance of the Last Supper was because of the example of Jesus and was believed to be in accordance with his command. We notice further that prayer and Bible study formed an important part of early Christian worship.

Organisation   We learn very little from the book of Acts about the internal problems of the local churches; we have to go to the epistles for information about this. But Acts does provide some information about the way the church was organised. The apostles played an important role. They were the obvious leaders of the emerging church. They soon recognised the need to split responsibilities, and another group was appointed to look after administration of relief schemes for widows (Acts 6), which enabled the apostles to concentrate on the work of spiritual leadership. Judas was replaced by Matthias, whose qualification for the office rested on the fact that he had been with Jesus and was a witness to his resurrection (Acts 1:21,22). Later Paul was to claim that he had been appointed an apostle by Christ and God the Father (Gal. 1:1).

In addition to apostles, we discover from Acts that elders were appointed: Paul and Barnabas certainly did this on their first missionary tour (Acts 14:23). No specific information is given regarding the function of these elders. It should be noted that the idea of elders may well have been taken over from Jewish practice, since a system of eldership was in existence in connection with the synagogues. If the church in this book seems rather disorganised and undeveloped, it should be remembered that the author's purpose is not to map the development of a system of church leaders, but to plot the progress of the preaching of the gospel from Jerusalem to Rome. Moreover, the greater emphasis given to the superintendence of the Holy Spirit in the early church serves to remind us that his activity is more important than any system of church officials.

The church in the epistles
A much more developed idea of the church is found in the epistles, especially in those of Paul.

Local and universal   The apostle sees the church as both a company of believers in a specific locality and as a universal body. Each epistle is addressed to a church or a group of churches (except the Pastorals and Philemon). In Ephesians and Colossians (Eph. 1:22; Col. 1:18), Paul expounds his view of Christ as Head of the church, that is, the whole church. Both of these aspects are important for a right understanding of Paul's view of the church. In his epistles he deals with each local church situation differently, never imposing a stereotyped pattern.

It seems likely that when Paul addressed a church in a certain locality, the community consisted of several house groups which together formed the church (compare Rom. 16:5,10,11). This is a natural extension of what happened on the day of Pentecost when the believers broke bread in their homes (Acts 2:46). It explains also some of the problems of communication which the early Christians faced, for there was clearly no one place where all the Christians could meet. The three thousand converted on the day of Pentecost at Jerusalem must have been distributed over a wide area.

Nevertheless, Paul has much to say about the unity of the church. He thinks of the community in terms of metaphors which can be understood only in a corporate sense. He uses the illustration of a *body* (Rom. 12:4–8; 1 Cor. 12:12–30), in which each part is essential to the proper function of the whole. He also writes of the community as a *building* in which, again, each section is interlocked with other sections to form a whole unit (1 Cor. 3:10; Eph. 2:19–22). He even describes the church as a *bride* (Eph. 5:25). In Ephesians 4 and Philippians 2, he makes the point that unity is essential for the Christian community.

Worship   We cannot deduce much from Paul's epistles about the worship procedures in the early churches, although there are some indirect indications. There is evidence that psalms and hymns and spiritual songs were used (Eph. 5:19). In addition, readings from Scripture and the exercise of spiritual gifts are mentioned in connection with the Corinthian church (1 Cor. 14:26). Public reading of scripture is also mentioned in 1 Timothy 4:13. At an early date there was evidently added the reading of letters such as Paul's (compare 1 Thess. 5:27; Col. 4:16), and later on presumably the reading of the Gospels, although we have no direct reference to this in Paul's epistles. The apostle assumes that corporate prayer would be practised (compare 1 Cor. 1:2). He himself gives us many samples of his own prayers, especially in the opening section of his letters. We know of no liturgical procedures as such, but we have some suggestions of statements of belief (as, for instance, 1 Cor. 15:3,4; or Rom. 10:9). It is natural to suppose that the early Christians would affirm their faith at various times when they met. In Romans 6:17 Paul refers to the standard of teaching which they had received, while in the Pastoral epistles there are several references to 'the truth' or 'the deposit', which suggests an agreed basis of doctrine. We cannot attribute to the New Testament church the same kind of basis of faith which Christians have used to define their position throughout the later history of the church. But it would be folly to suppose that the churches founded by Paul were not reasonably uniform in their understanding of what was basic to their Christian position.

The practice of baptism and the observance of the Lord's Supper was followed by Paul, as is clear especially from 1 Corinthians. Paul did not usually baptise his converts himself. Although recognising its importance, he considered that the work of preaching took precedence (1 Cor. 1:17). For Paul, baptism was regarded as the symbol of admittance to the church (compare 1 Cor. 12:13), but he directly connects it with the work of the Spirit. There is no question, therefore, of baptism having a magical function. In one passage – Romans 6 – Paul brings out the theological significance of baptism. He speaks of the transference from death to life in terms of baptism, and it is clear that he regards it as much more than a ritual act. The believer's life is seen to be closely connected with the life of the risen Lord.

Paul records that the details of the Lord's Supper had been passed on to him (1 Cor. 11:23–26). He considered it to be important to preserve the words which Jesus used when he instituted the Supper. There are some differences from the wording in the Gospels, the most significant of which is the emphasis in Paul's record on the Supper as a memorial. There can be no doubt that Paul understood from this that the Supper was to be repeated and this was presumably the opinion shared generally by the churches. From 1 Corinthians 10:17 it is clear that sharing in the Lord's Supper was regarded by Paul as an evidence of the unity of the church ('one body', 'one loaf'). It was also a focus for fellowship. It was because of the lack of such fellowship at Corinth that Paul had to criticise the church, for some were well fed and others were going hungry, a situation contrary to the spirit of the Lord's Supper.

Church leaders   When we consider the ministry of the church in Paul's epistles, we find many aspects which tie in with the book of Acts. The apostles are still important. Indeed, Paul goes to considerable lengths to demonstrate that God had appointed him as an apostle (Gal. 1:11–2:10). Apostles are mentioned as one of the gifts to the church (1 Cor. 12:28; Eph. 4:11). But it should be noted that Paul was not the only one to be called an apostle who did not belong to the original twelve (compare Barnabas, 1 Cor. 9:6). In his greeting to the Philippians (1:1) Paul mentions bishops and deacons. But the only other place where he mentions such offices is in the Pastoral epistles. In 1 Timothy 3:1–7 he outlines the qualities needed for the office of bishop, while in Titus 1:5–9 he speaks first of elders and then of bishops in a way which shows there is no clear distinction between the two offices. Indeed it seems best to regard 'bishops' as elders who performed special functions of oversight. There is no suggestion, however, that each local community had only one bishop.

The office of deacon is specifically mentioned and it is reasonable to see this as an office which is an extension of the kind of function performed by the seven men of Acts 6. It is noteworthy that high spiritual qualities are required for this office, as for the office of bishop. It is not clear whether deaconesses were generally appointed, but there is a possibility that 1 Timothy 3:11 may refer to such an order, although the wording could refer to deacons' wives. But in writing to Rome Paul mentions Phoebe, whom he describes as a deaconess (Rom. 16:1). There seems to be some indication of the work of women in the service of the church. Indeed, according to the Pastorals, widows, who could be of use and who were sixty years old or more, could be officially enrolled in church service (1 Tim. 5:9–16).

Spiritual gifts   Another important aspect of Paul's view of the church is his teaching on spiritual gifts. Most of his remarks on this subject are found in 1 Corinthians. It is not certain how far the problem of the gifts in that church was faced in other churches. It is reasonable to conclude that the problem was expressed in the most acute form in the Corinthian church. Paul devotes three chapters (12–14) to the problem, although chapter 13 may be described as an interlude, yet highly relevant. We may summarise Paul's teaching on spiritual gifts in the following way.

We note first that there was a wide variety. Sometimes Paul refers to gifts in terms of the functions of the recipients, such as *apostles, prophets, teachers, evangelists* (Eph. 4:11); sometimes in terms of personal qualities such as *discernment of spirits, faith, mercy;* and sometimes in terms of abilities, like *knowledge, tongues, interpretation, administration* (compare 1 Cor. 12:8–10; 28–30). The gifts, therefore, spread over the wide range of Christian activity. This suggests that they are to be considered normal, not abnormal.

The second feature to note is that the giver of the gifts is God. There is no suggestion that any of the gifts are earned, nor are they distributed by virtue of any merit in the recipient. The Spirit apportions individually as he wills (1 Cor. 12:11). This means that no one can pride himself on possessing any particular gift. It also means that Paul did not suppose that all Christians would possess and exercise all the gifts of the Spirit.

The third point to notice is that Paul does not give undue weight to any of the gifts, as if possession of them set the possessor in an advantageous position over others, with the exception of the office of an apostle. Those who are expected to exercise authority are presumably those who possess the gift of administration.

There is some difference of opinion among exponents of Paul's teaching as to the timing of the reception of the gifts. One school of thought takes the view that at conversion every believer receives the Spirit and therefore receives whatever gifts God chooses to bestow. Another school of thought maintains that the giving of the gifts is to be kept distinct from the conversion experience, and is generally linked with 'baptism in the Spirit'. But as we have noted earlier Paul does not speak of 'baptism' in the Spirit; he speaks of being 'filled' with the Spirit (for example, Eph. 5:18). His approach certainly leaves room for the development of spiritual gifts, but he does not specifically state that believers receive a special infilling subsequent to conversion.

Another matter of some dispute is whether the gifts of the Spirit are special developments of natural gifts or whether they are special endowments. Those who adopt the former view generally explain the phenomenon of tongues, on the basis of Acts 2, as being utterances in identifiable languages, while those preferring the latter view see tongues as a more ecstatic phenomenon. Whichever view is held, it does not conflict with the point mentioned above that all the gifts are God-given.

Women in the church   We cannot leave Paul's doctrine of the church without some reference to his view of the ministry of women. Although he urges women to be silent in church (1 Cor. 14:34–36; 1 Tim. 2:11), he generally has a high view of their place in ministering. In Galatians 3:28 he emphatically affirms that in

Christ there is 'neither male nor female', which suggests that men and women are to be regarded as of equal status. At the same time he does not permit women to exercise 'authority' over men (1 Tim. 2:12). He was evidently counteracting a tendency which was developing in the early church, presumably because women were abusing their new-found freedom in Christ. It should be noted also that Paul puts no obstacles in the way of women exercising the ministry of prayer or prophecy, even in public (1 Cor. 11:5).

It is noticeable that in the rest of the New Testament epistles there is not much information on the doctrine of the church. In the book of Hebrews there are no references to church officers, only a general reference to 'leaders' (Heb. 13:7,17). There are no clear references to the Lord's Supper, and two passing allusions to baptism (Heb. 6:2; 10:22). If the organisation of the church referred to in this epistle seems to be slight, it is paralleled in James, where the community is described in terms of the 'assembly' (Jas. 2:2) and where elders are mentioned in connection with a case of healing (Jas. 5:14). One aspect which is clearly brought out, however, is the fact that social position was to be allowed no weight in the church. The rich were not to have any advantage over the poor (Jas. 2:1–13), nor vice versa.

In 1 Peter the church is seen as *a redeemed community* (1 Pet. 1:18,19) and as a *building* (1 Pet. 2:4–8). It is also seen as *the people of God* (1 Pet. 2:9,10). Nothing is said about the organisation apart from the reference to elders in 1 Peter 5:1. It is worth noting that the title 'Bishop' is used, but is reserved for Christ himself (1 Pet. 2:25, AV). In the Johannine epistles the only reference to a church occurs in 3 John 9, but throughout these letters there is a strong underlying sense of community. It is only in the case of Diotrephes, who appears to be going beyond his rights in his exercise of authority, that John shows any interest in church matters.

The church in the book of Revelation

This book is more productive, not only in the letters to the seven churches of Asia, but also in the description of the church as a *bride*. The messages to the churches are intended to be representative, having both a local and an extended application. Each church has an 'angel', who may be a heavenly representative or an earthly leader. There is insufficient evidence to support the view that each 'angel' was a bishop. In fact little can be gleaned about church organisation. What is more important is the spiritual state of the churches, which clearly varied widely.

When the church is described as a 'bride' (Rev. 19:7,8; 21:9), it is evident that the description is meant to counterbalance the description of the 'harlot': the true church of God over against its satanic counterfeit. At the second coming of Christ the people of God are to be united with him in a way which can be pictured as the 'marriage supper of the Lamb'. This shows the church, not in its present state, but in its state of perfection and purity, the consummation of all that precedes.

14

THE
LAST THINGS

We have already seen that the gospel has much to say about the past (the historic mission of Jesus in dealing with the effect of man's sins) and the present (in the individual and in the church). Our attention must now be drawn to the New Testament teaching about the future and this focuses on three areas of interest – life after death, the second coming of Christ and the final judgement.

Life after death

A careful study of the Old Testament does not supply much information about life after death, but we find much more specific information in the New Testament. We must approach this subject with some reserve, for there is much that we would like to know which has not been revealed. There must inevitably remain an air of mystery over what happens after death.

We note first of all that there are three accounts in the Gospels of people being raised from the dead: Jairus' daughter, the widow's son at Nain, and Lazarus. These instances are notable because in no case do we have any account of the dead person's experience. The same is true of the raising to life of Dorcas by Peter (Acts 9:36–43) and of Eutychus by Paul (Acts 20:9–12). These instances demonstrate the possibility of bringing a dead person back to life, but tell us nothing about the state of existence after death. It is worth noting that in two of the instances cited from the Gospels, death is spoken of in terms of 'sleep', a familiar way of speaking of it in those days. Of paramount importance to the issue of life after death is the central fact of the resurrection of Jesus from the dead.

A bodily, but different, life   We may next enquire whether Jesus himself gave any indication of what life after death is like. One or two passages may throw some light on this subject. The Sadducees, who did not believe in the resurrection of the dead, tried to trap Jesus with a question about a woman who married a man and after his death married his brother (as the Levitical laws required), repeating the process as far as the seventh brother (Mark 12:18–27). The Sadducees wanted to know whose wife she would be in the resurrection. This gave Jesus an opportunity to show that an understanding of the afterlife on the basis of a continuation of this life is invalid. The idea of marriage is ruled out. Discussions about status are therefore entirely inappropriate. Jesus' comment about the patriarchs suggests that they are still alive, since God is 'God of the living, not of the dead'. In another passage Jesus speaks of the patriarchs sharing a meal with the 'many' who come from east and west (Matt. 8:11,12), which suggests some kind of bodily resurrection.

A passage which poses some difficulties, but which nevertheless throws light on the afterlife, is the case of the rich man and Lazarus (Luke 16:19–31). This story would make no sense if some conscious existence in the afterlife were not a reality. But the details must not be too rigidly pressed. Nevertheless it is inescapable that behaviour in this life will, in some way, affect one's status in the afterlife.

'Paradise'   One other passage which is relevant here is Jesus' answer to the dying man on the cross, in which he assured the man that he would be with him 'in Paradise' that very day. (Luke 23:42,43). Elsewhere in the New Testament 'Paradise' seems to be used to denote heaven (2 Cor. 12:3; Rev. 2:7), and probably does so here. In this case what is most evident about Paradise is that it is in the presence of Christ. Although nothing is said about the form of existence, it is significant in view of other New Testament evidence that attention is focused on the presence of Christ.

A future resurrection   In the account of the raising of Lazarus, Jesus makes the statement, 'I am the resurrection and the life' (John 11:25), which shows that the idea of resurrection is closely linked with the person of Jesus and with his own resurrection. This leads us to suppose that some connection with the resurrection body of Jesus may be in mind. In John 5:25–29, Jesus refers to 'a resurrection of life' and 'a resurrection of judgement', which draws a distinction between the destiny of those doing good and those doing evil. We note that all will be involved in a future resurrection, although no information is given about the resurrection state. The post-resurrection life which believers will experience is frequently described in John's Gospel as 'eternal life'.

We have already noted the two cases of people raised from the dead in Acts. We need also to note that when Stephen died he is said to have 'fallen asleep' (Acts 7:60). But the nature of the book as a whole does not lend itself to discussions on the afterlife.

The resurrection body   When we come to Paul's letters we find more specific reference to various aspects of the afterlife. Paul's main discussion of the resurrection theme is in 1 Corinthians 15. He certainly links the resurrection of believers with the resurrection of Christ. But he also discusses the question of the resurrection body (1 Cor. 15:35). In answering this question, he pursues two lines of thought. First he uses an *analogy between Adam and Christ*: the former was a natural man, 'from the earth, a man of dust'. The latter is a life-giving Spirit 'from heaven' (1 Cor. 15:45–48). Paul affirms also that, just as we have resembled Adam in terms of living an earthly life, so we shall resemble Christ in living a heavenly life.

In developing the idea of the resurrection body, he uses the *analogy of the seed* (1 Cor. 15:35–44). He points out that different seeds have different forms of existence, but the particular form of existence is perfectly suited to the nature of each seed. He uses this to illustrate that a spiritual being will be clothed in a spiritual body. This implies that there will be a radical transformation. Such a change is, in fact, also explicitly stated in Philippians 3:21, where our 'lowly body' is said to be transformed to Christ's 'glorious body' at his appearing.

It is in 2 Corinthians 5:1–10 that Paul expounds this theme in greater detail. There are many difficulties in this passage, but certain facts stand out. Paul cannot bear the thought of being 'naked'. He is thinking of the believer's state when the earthly 'tent' is destroyed, that is, the physical body at death. But he does not enlarge on the subject of the resurrection body. He is wanting to assure his readers that when they are away from, or without, the body, they will be present with the Lord (2 Cor. 5:8). This is a deep conviction with the apostle. In Philippians 1:23, he equates 'departing' with 'being with Christ'. In doing so he helps to explain the meaning of Jesus' promise to the dying criminal.

It is impossible to say with certainty when, in Paul's thought, the believer receives the resurrection body. If it is at death, this would imply a constant sequence of resurrections, and seems to conflict with the idea of a resurrection 'day'. One attempt to solve the problem is to appeal to a different awareness of time in the afterlife and to suppose that the believer at death is at once aware of the resurrection day. This idea is difficult. It seems better to say that the believer is immediately in God's presence and that at the end he will have received a resurrection body, but neither Paul nor any other New Testament writers provide clear evidence as to when this happens.

Other New Testament writers do, however, throw some further light on this subject. In Hebrews 12:22,23 there is reference to a heavenly scene in which the spirits of 'just men made perfect' are present. This may suggest a bodiless state of existence. But the passage is not dealing with the resurrection body, but with heavenly worship and the perfection of the worshippers. In 1 Peter there are two difficult statements which may refer to the afterlife (3:19; 4:6), but the interpretation of these statements is not certain. Neither of them throws any light on the resurrection body. In the book of Revelation, which deals so specifically with the future, there are a few statements which require mention. There is a reference to martyrs 'under the altar' (Rev. 6:9), which must be taken to mean 'in the presence of God'. Their cry for vindication shows further that they are fully conscious of what they are asking for. Another feature of this book is the fact that the saints are said to be clothed in white linen (Rev. 7:13,14), symbolic of righteousness, although nothing is said about their resurrection bodies. There is little specific information about the afterlife itself, although various rewards are promised to those who conquer in this life (Rev. 2:7,11,17,26; 3:5,12,21). There are differences of interpretation of the two resurrections in Revelation 20, but there is no dispute that a general resurrection will take place at the close of the present age.

The future coming of Christ

The climax of history   The New Testament sees the present age as the *age of the church* or the *age of the kingdom*. We are now living in the last days and this period will culminate in the return of

Christ. This second coming of Christ is therefore the climax of history. We need to note the main sources of our information about this event and we shall then discuss its importance for our understanding of New Testament teaching as a whole.

Jesus certainly taught that he, as Son of Man, would come again (Matt. 16:27). He uses several different figures of speech to describe the coming. It would be a glorious event. It would be 'on the clouds of heaven' and 'with a loud trumpet call' (Matt. 24:30,31), which shows its public character. Both the glory and the clouds are paralleled in Daniel 7:13,14.

Signs of the coming   Moreover, the coming of Jesus will be preceded by signs, enumerated in Mark 13, Matthew 24 and 25 and Luke 21. The signs mentioned are of various types. Some are disturbances among people (wars, persecutions), some natural disasters (earthquakes, famines), some signs in the heavens affecting the sun and moon, and at least one relating to the gospel (it was to be preached to all nations).

These signs have all been partially fulfilled at different stages of the history of the church, but prior to the coming of Jesus they will presumably be intensified. This highlights a difficulty which arises over the time of the coming, for Jesus Christ disclaimed knowledge of when it would be (Mark 13:32), and said that only the Father knew the precise timetable. Moreover, he gave repeated exhortations to the disciples to be on the watch because the coming would be as unexpected as that of a thief. The parable of the virgins illustrates this point (Matt. 25:1–13), and ends with advice to the disciples to be ready for his return, since they do not know when it will be. This curious mixture of surprise and suddenness, mixed with events which must happen first, seems paradoxical, but the explanation must be that Jesus wanted the believers to be in a state of continual preparedness, but also cautioned against supposing that the coming had already happened, as some were later to claim.

When we turn to the fourth Gospel we find no such explicit references to the future coming of Christ. Yet there is no reason to conclude that different teaching is involved. John 14:3 makes clear the fact that Jesus will come again, although nowhere in this Gospel is the manner of coming mentioned. There is no reference, for instance, to clouds. But this feature occurs again in Acts 1:11, where the return of Jesus is likened to his ascension (he vanished into a cloud). This early reference to a future coming is not, however, repeated in this book. It may be said that both John and Acts are preoccupied with other themes.

In Paul's epistles, on the other hand, the references are much more numerous. Indeed, Paul uses several different words to describe the event – the 'coming', the 'revelation', the 'appearing'. He also writes about the 'day of the Lord', which shows he is thinking of a specific event which will bring the present age to a close. In 1 Thessalonians 4:13–5:11 he refers to the coming in terms very similar to those used by Jesus. He mentions the cry of command and the archangel's call, which are not referred to in the Gospels, but he includes reference to the trumpet sound and the clouds, as Jesus had done.

Suddenness of the return   Paul also mentions that the day of the Lord will come 'as a thief' (1 Thess. 5:2,4). It is evident that he had already told the Thessalonians about the coming of Jesus (compare 1 Thess. 5:1), which suggests that he made a practice of doing this when establishing his churches. It was a part of the essential message of the gospel. Yet he mentions it more specifically in 1 Thessalonians because of a misunderstanding which had arisen concerning it. Some of the believers had died since Paul's visit to the city, and the Christians could not work out what the position of these would be when Jesus came. Paul answers that those who had died would be in a position no different from those who are still alive. Both groups will be with the Lord. It is only in this passage that the apostle mentions the catching up of believers (commonly known as 'the rapture'). It connects with what Jesus said about the suddenness of his return; for example, there may be two men in the field and two women at the mill, of whom one will suddenly be taken and the other left behind (Matt. 24:40,41). Neither passage tells us anything more about the 'rapture', nor is there any information elsewhere in the New Testament about it.

Imminent, but not yet   We find the same tension in Paul between the conviction that the coming could happen at any time and the realisation that certain significant events must happen first, as we have already seen in the Gospels. In 2 Thessalonians 2:3 Paul points out that 'the man of lawlessness' must come to power first, and by this he evidently means a special manifestation of lawlessness. His reason for mentioning this is because some in Thessalonica had ceased working at their everyday jobs, so as to be ready for the coming. Paul realises that they had misunderstood the imminent aspect of the coming. He also mentions the 'restrainer' in this passage and there has been difference of opinion over the interpretation of this. It would appear most natural to suppose that Paul had the Roman State in mind, since during that period the State had succeeded in maintaining peace and political evils had less opportunity to be rampant. Nevertheless, we cannot exclude the probability that Paul was looking beyond contemporary political forces to spiritual agencies.

Other passages in which Paul refers to the coming should be mentioned. In Romans 13:12 he declares that 'the day is at hand'. In Philippians 3:20 he maintains that 'we await a Saviour' from heaven. In 1 Corinthians 15:24,25 Paul refers to the end as the time in which Jesus will deliver the kingdom to the Father, after having overcome all his enemies. The importance of the Lord's return for Paul cannot be over–emphasised. He sees it as the culminating event of human history. In the passage in Romans he shows that belief that this day is approaching should have an effect over the Christian's behaviour.

In Hebrews 9:28, we find the only description of the coming of Christ in the New Testament as the 'second', which links it closely with the 'first' (that is, the incarnation). The writer of this epistle assumes that he and his readers are already in the last days (Heb. 1:2), and he mentions the approach of 'the Day', by which he means the concluding event. Similarly, James (5:8) mentions that the coming of the Lord is at hand and uses this to urge suitable behaviour patterns. As in Hebrews, there is mention of 'the last days' (Jas. 5:3); in fact, James (5:9) refers to the Judge as already 'standing at the doors'. In Peter's two epistles we find the same emphasis on the imminence of the coming (compare 1 Pet. 4:7; 2 Pet. 3:3); but it is in the book of Revelation that the clearest teaching occurs.

The returning Lord in the book of Revelation   Since the book of Revelation is specifically about the end time, it is not surprising that more is said on a future coming. We shall note first the actual description of the coming which occurs in Revelation 19:11,12 (although 'coming' is not a precise term here, for the passage speaks of a manifestation; nevertheless, it is certainly the same event to which other passages have pointed). Christ is portrayed as a glorious warrior with flaming eyes, white robe and sword. He comes from heaven and is clearly highly exalted. He bears names like 'Faithful', 'True', 'Word of God', 'King of kings' and 'Lord of lords'. The picture is not of a Saviour, but of a Judge. So powerful is he that he subdues his enemies merely with the sword

135

from his mouth, that is, the words he speaks. He is accompanied by armies which do not need to fight. It is a scene of complete victory and marks the climax of history, since this appearance occurs at the end after the total destruction of the 'harlot Babylon' and before the judgement scene at the great white throne.

At the beginning of the book, the nearness of the end is announced (Rev. 1:1–3). This is presumably to remind the readers that what is written is relevant to them. It also shows that the whole book, including the messages to the churches, is to be considered from the point of view of the end events. Hence the coming of Christ is seen to be intricately connected, not only with the various scenes of judgement, but also with the worship passages which intersperse these scenes. There are several events which must happen before the second coming. The sequence of seals, trumpets and bowls are probably to be regarded as parallel series, each of which approaches the end along a different route. The total impression is one of inexorable justice. The forces of darkness, headed by 'antichrist', are seen having their final fling, but the issue is never in doubt. The 'warrior Lamb' is totally victorious.

When we enquire into the significance for the coming of the recurring worship passages, we discover that the main themes of those passages are the power and the justice of God, with an important emphasis also on the redemptive work which he has accomplished in Christ (compare Rev. 5:9). The Christ who comes in judgement is the Christ who has redeemed. The 'warrior Lamb' is 'the Lamb who was slain'. The coming is, therefore, seen to be the consummation of the entire mission of God in Christ. It is the only fitting conclusion to God's plan of salvation.

Some mention must be made of the connection between the future coming of Christ and the 'millennium'. The key passage is Revelation 20, but this passage has given rise to different interpretations. Some have taken the view that the coming inaugurates the reign of Christ on earth for 1,000 years. Another view is that his reign will be ushered in only when the gospel has been preached throughout the world. And yet a third view sees the present church era, from the ascension to the coming, as the reign of Christ, and takes the 1,000 years as symbolic rather than literal. There are difficulties with all these views, but the lack of clarity should warn us against too readily regarding views about the millennium as a test of orthodoxy.

Judgement

The idea that there will be a day of reckoning at the end of the present age is strongly supported in the New Testament. We have already seen that when Christ comes it will be to judge. Our task here is to show that judgement is as much a part of the revelation of God's character as is his mercy.

A great assize   There are references to 'the day of judgement' in the teaching of Jesus (Matt. 10:15; 11:22–24; 12:36). These allusions seem to point ahead to a great assize at which all will appear. Jesus condemned a spirit of judgemental superiority in his followers (Matt. 7:1,2). Several things, such as anger, are said to be culpable. Matthew records Jesus' saying that men would have to give account even for their careless words (Matt. 12:36), although he does not say when this will take place. Condemnation is pronounced on those who rob the poor, however 'legally' (Mark 12:40). We must conclude, therefore, that some kind of reckoning day is integral to Jesus' teaching about the future.

The basis of judgement   One passage from that teaching which is particularly relevant is Matthew 25:31–46, about the sheep and the goats. The setting is a great assize established by the Son of Man on his return in glory. That there is a clear-cut distinction between the two groups suggests a clear basis for such a division, and indeed this is stated in the passage. The test is the way in which each has reacted to the 'brethren'. If the 'brethren' are the followers of Jesus, judgement is made on the basis of the approach adopted towards Christians. But this may be understood either of nations or of individuals. The judgement on the 'goats' is seen to be wholly on the basis that they did *not* do good works to the King's brethren. This raises a problem, since it seems to regard good works as all-important, and it is not immediately apparent how this fits in with the mission of Christ on man's behalf. If everyone is going to be judged on the basis of works, why was the death of Christ necessary? We cannot suppose that this passage goes against the New Testament evidence as a whole and it must, therefore, be maintained that what is being judged is not the basis of salvation, but the working out of faith in social concern. It should be noted that, although the sheep are described as 'righteous' (Matt. 25:37), there is no suggestion that their righteousness was earned.

Christ as Judge   Although in John's Gospel Jesus states that he did not come to judge but to save (John 12:47), some teaching

137

about judgement is certainly included. Indeed, Jesus claims that the Father has given authority to the Son to judge (John 5:22,27). There is no contradiction here, for the former statement relates to Jesus' earthly life, whereas the latter refers to the final judgement. Not only is Jesus seen as Judge, but also as the basis of judgement. There is condemnation for those who do not believe in Jesus (John 3:18). Compromise is impossible, for a man either does or does not believe. In view of this emphasis in John's Gospel, it may be wondered how judgement on man's sin connects with judgement for unbelief in Jesus. They are not mutually exclusive. The concept of a holy God implies a condemnation on all that is unholy, for holiness cannot have anything to do with unholiness. This holds for both Old Testament and New Testament, but in the New Testament era there is the additional criterion of a person's attitude to Christ, who is the perfect example of a holy person. Jesus speaks of his cross as being related to man's judgement ('now is the judgement of this world' John 12:31), although he does not rule out a future judgement. Believers may know now how the world will stand in the future judgement. It has already been condemned.

The theme of judgement comes into Peter's speech in Cornelius' house (Acts 10:42), and in Paul's speech at Athens (Acts 17:30,31). In both cases Christ is the one who is ordained to be Judge. It was the reality of judgement and condemnation of sin that provided the background against which the early Christians exhorted people to repent.

Paul's enlargement on the theme of judgement shows how important it was in his teaching. Because God is righteous, unrighteous behaviour merits his wrath. It is revealed alongside his righteousness (Rom. 1:17,18). The one is as essential a part of his nature as the other. But judgement is also an essential part of wrath. Paul's view of salvation is that God has redeemed man from his wrath (Rom. 5:9), which means that those not covered by this salvation are answerable directly to God and will face condemnation. Paul has no doubt that on the day he judges, God's judgement will be absolutely fair, because he will even take people's secrets into account (Rom. 2:16). Jesus Christ is also linked with the act of judgement.

In Paul's view there are no exemptions from judgement. All men fall under the same condemnation (Rom. 5:18). Moreover, the apostle does not hesitate to use strong words like 'destruction' (1 Thess. 5:3) and 'perdition' (2 Thess. 2:3), when referring to the destiny of the ungodly, that is, those who have chosen to live without God. On the other hand, his doctrine of justification has a direct bearing on the theme of judgement, for he makes clear that for those 'in' Christ Jesus there is no longer any condemnation (Rom. 8:1). In other words the verdict of 'guilty' has already been pronounced, but because Christ has already taken the punishment a pardon is at once given to the believer.

The 'judgement seat'   This brings us to the theme of 'the judgement seat', and the question at once arises whether Paul drew a distinction between 'the judgement seat of Christ' and 'the judgement seat of God'. The former he specifically mentions in 2 Corinthians 5:10, in a passage in which he discusses the resurrection body. In the course of his statement he makes clear that everyone will receive a reward or punishment appropriate to what he has done in the course of his life. In another passage (Rom. 14:10) he refers as specifically to the judgement seat of God. There seems no reason to maintain that Paul thought of two judgement seats. It is a familiar thing for him to attribute to Jesus Christ what he also attributes to God (for example, creation, salvation). The difference in terminology, therefore, has no significance. It is likely that Paul thinks of the events at the judgement seat of Christ as taking place on the day of judgement at the end of the present age.

Reward   The apostle has much to say about rewards but the most specific passage to this effect is 1 Corinthians 3:12–15, in which he is comparing different ways in which people build a superstructure on the same foundation. Some are lasting, others are of only transient value. In the latter case real loss is involved, but not salvation. It is clear that Paul draws a distinction between salvation and rewards. Nevertheless, it must be noted that rewards are spiritual. Paul talks about the 'crown of life'. All in all it would seem clear that he thinks of individual acts of judgement in the present culminating in a final day of judgement in the future.

The epistle to the Hebrews makes the clear point that after death there is judgement (Heb. 9:27), although it gives no indication of the timing of the judgement. Another passage speaks of the fearful prospect of judgement (Heb. 10:27), which is not surprising in an epistle which refers to God as a 'consuming fire' (Heb. 12:29). Yet for believers the prospect is not devastating since this same epistle says so much about the intercession of Christ on their behalf. Some understanding of judgement, however, is regarded as a basic tenet of belief, according to Hebrews 6:1,2. In this case it is described as 'eternal'. According to James 5:9, the judge is already 'standing at the doors', but it would seem from the context that this must relate to the future. Peter writes about judgement beginning with the household of God (1 Pet. 4:17), and then goes on to compare this with the judgement of those who do not obey the gospel. There is much about judgement in 2 Peter and Jude, and examples are cited – like Sodom and Gomorrah (Jude 7; 2 Pet. 2:6) and the fallen angels (Jude 6; 2 Pet. 2:4). The idea of destruction in 2 Peter 3:7–10 is extended to the destruction of the present heaven and earth by fire.

It is, however, in the book of Revelation that the theme of judgement is most evident. The different sequences of seals, trumpets and bowls all concentrate on different aspects of judgement. The climax is reached when the fall of Babylon is announced (Rev. 17) and a dirge song is included (Rev. 18) to heighten the effect. But the real focal point is the description of the 'great white throne' in Revelation 20:11–15. This throne of judgement appears after the coming of Christ and at the dissolution of the present heaven and earth. A distinction is made between the position of believers and unbelievers, since the basis of judgement is whether or not names are written in 'the book of life'. But another 'book' is mentioned which records what people have done, and this must be understood, as far as believers are concerned, to relate to rewards. Although the Judge in this final scene is God, there is no reason to suppose that the judgement scene differs from that of the judgement seat of Christ.

Future destiny
The theme of judgement naturally leads to some consideration of the subsequent status of believers and non-believers, and for this we must gather up the main teaching in the New Testament on heaven and hell.

With Christ   The destiny of those 'in Christ' is to be with him in the presence of God. In the New Testament the presence of God is often described as heaven. Heaven is God's dwelling. Frequently God is addressed as 'in heaven' (compare the Lord's Prayer and the prayer of Matt. 11:25). Heaven is linked with the fatherhood of God. These points remind us that heaven is not to be regarded as a locality. Some references might perhaps lead to the assumption that it is, as, for instance, when Jesus is said to have been 'taken up' into heaven (Acts 1:11). Certainly, the Christians became convinced that Jesus had ascended to 'the right hand of God' (compare Heb. 1:3). Being 'in heaven' and being 'in the presence of God' are synonymous. When Paul speaks of his own experience in being 'caught up to the third heaven' (2 Cor. 12:2), it seems clear that he is thinking of the presence of God.

In community   In Paul's view the believer's true home, his 'commonwealth' is in heaven (Phil. 3:20). That heaven was also seen in terms of community is shown by the concept of the new Jerusalem in Galatians 4:26; Hebrews 12:22–24 and Revelation 21 and 22. It may seem incongruous that the heavenly community idea should be expressed in terms of a city, which is a man-made concept, but the illustration strongly brings out the sense of organised togetherness which is characteristic of heaven.

Hell and punishment   There is no denying that Jesus spoke of hell in connection with punishment (for example, Matt. 11:23; Luke 16:23). The idea is often linked with fire (Mark 9:43) and this is undoubtedly intended symbolically, as it is in Revelation 19 and 20. 'Hell', in New Testament language, certainly implies exclusion from the presence of God, whatever else we make of the idea of punishment (compare 2 Thess. 1:9). In this respect it is the antithesis of 'paradise'. Although the New Testament is reserved about the final destiny of unbelievers, a clear distinction is made which cannot be glossed over. In many parts of the New Testament the inevitability of judgement on unbelievers is stressed and there is no suggestion that subsequent to this life any who do not believe will have a second chance to respond in faith. In the final consummation not only death, but also Hades, are themselves destroyed (Rev. 20:14).

15

CONCLUSION

In this brief survey of New Testament teaching we have noted a remarkable consistency throughout the various books. There is a common understanding of the gospel. Man's basic need is everywhere apparent and God's gracious provision in Christ knits the various strands into a whole. Christians are provided with a clear understanding of God's holy nature and of his provision of a means for reconciling people to himself. There is a consistent presentation of the exalted nature of Jesus Christ linked with the indisputable fact that he was a real man.

The New Testament is rich in its description of the activities of the Holy Spirit and shows his indwelling presence to be indispensable for the Christian life. All the emphasis on being 'in Christ' or 'in the Spirit' point to the exalted quality of life which Christians inherit.

This new quality of life cannot, however, be developed in isolation. The New Testament has a clear teaching about the value and responsibilities of the church. Fellowship with other believers is to provide the environment in which the fruits of the gospel are intended to be seen.

Whereas we would like to know all about the future, the New Testament teaching is sufficient to inform us of what we need to know, although holding us in some suspense over the nature of the blessedness and glory which is promised to those in Christ. Solemn warnings are also included for unbelievers.

It is hoped that the brief treatments of the various themes discussed will stimulate many to seek further explorations into the rich deposits of truth which God has embedded in his word.